SpringerBriefs in Offending Populations & Correctional Psychotherapy

Series Editor

Karla Sapp, Midway, USA

SpringerBriefs in Offending Populations & Correctional Psychotherapy is a series of compact, high-quality volumes dealing with all aspects of the American carceral system and offender populations, from identifying systemic issues of the prison system to addressing services needed to support offender mental health.

Featuring concise titles between 50-125 pages, the cross-disciplinary series incorporates research and policy suggestions spanning mental health, criminal justice, and more, including topics such as correctional psychology and counseling, transformative and restorative justice, recidivism and rehabilitation, advocacy and public policy issues, and dismantling prison pipelines.

SpringerBriefs in Offending Populations & Correctional Psychotherapy will be of interest to a broad range of researchers and practitioners working in offender and prison research and in related academic fields such as Psychology, Counseling, Criminology, Criminal Justice, and Law.

Chanda Williams

Yoga in Prisons

An Analysis of the Perceived Long-term Effects of Trauma-Informed, Mindfulness-Based Yoga for Incarcerated Populations

Springer

Chanda Williams
Pacifica Graduate Institute
Oakland, CA, USA

ISSN 2731-8966 ISSN 2731-8974 (electronic)
SpringerBriefs in Offending Populations & Correctional Psychotherapy
ISBN 978-3-031-98367-2 ISBN 978-3-031-98368-9 (eBook)
https://doi.org/10.1007/978-3-031-98368-9

This Springer imprint is published by the registered company Springer Nature Switzerland AG
The registered company address is: Gewerbestrasse 11, 6330 Cham, Switzerland

Acknowledgments

I offer my deepest gratitude to the incarcerated men who shared their stories, their vulnerability, and their wisdom with me. This work is possible because of your courage, your honesty, and your refusal to let systems define your humanity. Thank you for trusting me with your experiences and for allowing yoga to become a space of breath, agency, and connection.

I extend my heartfelt appreciation to my teachers, mentors, and colleagues who nurtured my growth as a researcher and yoga therapist. Your guidance helped me hold the complexities of this work with rigor, compassion, and integrity.

I am grateful to my family and loved ones who supported me through the labor of this project. Your encouragement sustained me through every challenge and every moment of doubt.

This work was supported by the UCSF Osher Center research and fellowship programs (NCCIH T35 T35AT010592, MPI: Chao and Adler; T32 AT003997, MPI: Hecht and Adler). Their support made it possible to deepen this inquiry into trauma-responsive care and integrative health equity.

May this book honor the brilliance, resilience, and dignity of justice-impacted people everywhere, and may it serve as a small contribution toward the collective work of healing and liberation.

Competing Interests The author has no competing interests to declare that are relevant to the content of this manuscript.

Contents

About the Author

Chanda Williams is an integrative health equity researcher, trauma-informed yoga therapist, and scholar dedicated to expanding access to culturally grounded, trauma-responsive healing practices for justice-impacted communities. She began her academic journey with a BS in mechanical engineering, a foundation that deepened her curiosity about systems, structures, and the mechanics of the human body. She later earned a PhD in depth psychology, with an emphasis on somatic studies, and is a certified yoga therapist with more than twenty years of teaching experience. Dr. Williams's research centers on the lived experiences of incarcerated people, the impact of yoga therapy on wellbeing, and community-driven models of collective healing and liberation. For more than twenty years, Dr. Williams has taught yoga in diverse communities, including jails and prisons in California, where she supports people in reclaiming agency, embodiment, and wellbeing. She is currently a postdoctoral research fellow at the University of California, San Francisco, where she studies integrative health approaches for marginalized and justice-impacted populations.

Chapter 1
Introduction

"...all over the world, the institution of the prison serves as a place to warehouse people who represent major social problems... prison serves as an institution that consolidates the state's inability and refusal to address the most pressing social problems of this era."

Angela Y. Davis, Freedom is a Constant Struggle: Ferguson, Palestine and the Foundations of a Movement [1]

1.1 Two Worlds: Yoga in the Contemporary West and Yoga in Prisons

Yoga, in its modern Western incarnation, has flourished as a wellness industry spanning boutique studios, corporate wellness programs, and high-end gym chains. It is a practice marketed for stress relief, physical fitness, and personal transformation, often commodified into an accessible, palatable form detached from its spiritual and philosophical roots. In contrast, yoga in prisons operates in an environment antithetical to peace and self-liberation—spaces defined by confinement, surveillance, and systemic neglect. This chapter explores these two worlds, illustrating the stark contrast between yoga as a commercialized practice in the contemporary West and its presence as a radical act of body autonomy and reclamation in the prison system.

1.1.1 Yoga in the West: Wellness, Affluence, and Accessibility

Over the past century, yoga has transformed from an esoteric Eastern spiritual discipline into a multi-billion-dollar wellness enterprise in the West [2, 3]. Contemporary yoga classes cater to various demographics, from stressed-out professionals to

C. Williams, *Yoga in Prisons*, SpringerBriefs in Offending Populations & Correctional Psychotherapy, https://doi.org/10.1007/978-3-031-98368-9_1

fitness enthusiasts, new mothers, and retirees. Studios offer a range of options—hot yoga, power yoga, aerial yoga, and restorative yoga—each tailored to specific physical and mental health benefits. High-end studios in urban centers boast sleek interiors, ambient lighting, and heated floors, providing an atmosphere of tranquility that encourages mindfulness and self-care. In corporate offices, yoga is introduced as a productivity tool, a means to combat workplace stress, improve focus, and reduce absenteeism. Within gyms, yoga is packaged as an athletic endeavor, with classes emphasizing flexibility, core strength, and weight loss.

This commodification of yoga in the West often strips the practice of its deeper philosophical and spiritual dimensions, reducing it to a lifestyle accessory [4, 5]. The commercialization is evident in the billion-dollar yoga apparel industry, where luxury brands sell high-performance leggings and eco-friendly mats, reinforcing the exclusivity of yoga as a practice for the privileged. The archetypal image of a yoga practitioner—young, slim, affluent, and often white—dominates media representation, shaping public perception of what yoga is and who it is for.

Yet, for all its popularity in the West, yoga in these settings is largely elective, pursued by individuals seeking self-improvement, relaxation, or community. It is a practice of choice, framed within the realm of personal wellness and self-care. The spaces in which yoga is practiced—quiet, controlled, aesthetically pleasing—foster an environment of ease and comfort, supporting introspection and embodiment. This is a stark contrast to yoga's presence in the carceral system, where the very conditions of incarceration are antithetical to healing.

1.1.2 Yoga in Prisons: A Radical Reclamation of Humanity

Incarceration is the embodiment of deprivation, and the prison system is designed to strip individuals of autonomy, self-expression, and connection to the body and mind [6–9]. Harsh fluorescent lights, overcrowded cells, constant surveillance, and the ever-present threat of violence define daily life. In the United States, there are currently 1.8 million people incarcerated in prisons and jails [10]. The carceral environment fosters disembodiment—many incarcerated individuals experience chronic stress, dissociation, and trauma responses that sever their connection to themselves and their surroundings. In such a space, yoga becomes an act of resistance, a reclaiming of agency in a system that seeks to dehumanize.

Unlike yoga studios, prisons do not offer serene spaces with dim lighting and essential oil diffusers. Instead, yoga is often practiced on cold, hard concrete floors, in multipurpose rooms, or even within cramped cells. Access to yoga programs is inconsistent and largely dependent on external facilitators—often nonprofit organizations or volunteer teachers—who navigate complex institutional barriers to offer classes. Participants may not have access to mats, proper attire, or even a quiet space, yet they practice regardless, demonstrating resilience in the face of adversity.

For incarcerated individuals, yoga is not a leisure activity; it is a survival strategy. Studies have shown that trauma-informed yoga in prisons reduces stress, improves emotional regulation, and fosters a sense of self-worth among participants [11–15]. Many individuals in the prison system have extensive histories of trauma—physical abuse, neglect, racialized violence, and systemic oppression [16–26]. The body, for many, has been a site of harm and punishment rather than healing. Yoga offers a rare opportunity for self-soothing and reconnection, a chance to inhabit the body with compassion rather than fear. The physical postures and breathwork help mitigate the effects of chronic stress and trauma [12–15, 27–29]. Deep breathing activates the parasympathetic nervous system, countering the heightened state of vigilance that incarceration induces. Movements such as gentle stretching and grounding postures provide a sense of stability, an embodied reminder that the individual still possesses control over their body in a space designed to strip them of it.

Beyond physiological benefits, yoga in prisons fosters a shift in self-perception. Incarceration erodes identity, reducing individuals to numbers, case files, and criminal records [11–13]. Yoga restores a sense of personhood and encourages self-reflection, emotional regulation, and the possibility of transformation. Some incarcerated individuals become yoga teachers themselves, extending the practice to others within the prison system, creating micro-communities of healing within spaces of confinement [30].

1.1.3 Origins of Yoga

Rooted in the ancient spiritual traditions of the Indian subcontinent, yoga is a multifaceted practice that integrates breath, movement, ethics, meditation, and philosophy. Far beyond a physical exercise regimen, yoga emerged as a path toward liberation—moksha—designed to cultivate clarity, compassion, discipline, and unity between body, mind, and spirit. Classical texts such as the Yoga Sutras of Patanjali, the Bhagavad Gita, and the Hatha Yoga Pradipika illuminate yoga's ethical foundations (yamas and niyamas), contemplative practices (dhyana), and physiological disciplines (asana and pranayama) as interdependent tools for self-realization and collective harmony. Traditionally taught in relational, lineage-based settings, yoga was never meant to be extracted from its cultural context or commodified as a wellness trend.

Over time, however, as yoga spread globally, particularly into Western settings, its meanings and methods have shifted. Contemporary yoga in the West is often associated with physical postures and marketed for stress relief, fitness, or flexibility, frequently divorced from its philosophical roots. Yet in parallel, a growing body of scientific research in Western medicine has begun to affirm what traditional yogic systems have long known: that mind-body practices like yoga can support physical health, mental well-being, and nervous system regulation. Studies have linked yoga to improvements in cardiovascular health, reductions in anxiety and depression, and enhanced emotional resilience—especially in trauma-affected populations. As yoga continues to evolve, an opportunity emerges to honor its origins while integrating its healing potential within holistic and justice-centered frameworks of care.

1.1.4 Cultural Misappropriation

Cultural misappropriation occurs when healing practices from historically marginalized or colonized communities are extracted from their original cultural, spiritual, or communal contexts and repackaged for profit, power, or prestige, often without acknowledgment, permission, or reciprocity. In the context of yoga, cultural misappropriation is particularly pervasive. Practices that were once sacred, relational, and interwoven with philosophy and ethics have been commodified and stripped of their deeper meaning. Yoga has been marketed and consumed largely by white, affluent populations, often reinforcing systems of privilege and exclusion while ignoring the ongoing struggles of the communities from which these teachings originate. True integrative health must be grounded in humility, equity, and cultural respect, not appropriation or exploitation. This means actively challenging biomedical dominance, commercialism, and erasure while elevating the lived expertise of traditional healers and lineage holders.

As yoga becomes further embedded in Western medical and wellness frameworks, it is essential to examine how power, capitalism, and colonial legacies shape whose voices are centered and whose are ignored. Cultural misappropriation in yoga does not only distort the practice, it causes harm by continuing cycles of extraction and invisibility. Yoga as a liberatory practice calls for a shift from appropriation to appreciation through a framework of cultural humility, which includes self-reflection, accountability, and ongoing dialogue with the communities we serve and learn from. For practitioners, facilitators, and researchers working in prisons or any institutional setting, this means moving beyond performative inclusion toward deep, relational integrity—ensuring that yoga and other healing modalities are taught and shared in ways that honor their roots and serve collective liberation.

1.1.5 Moving Towards Acknowledgment and Appreciation

Moving toward true appreciation of yoga's origins requires a shift from passive participation to conscious acknowledgment. This begins with understanding yoga not merely as a set of physical postures but as a deeply philosophical, spiritual, and ethical system rooted in South Asian culture. Honoring yoga's origins means learning about the historical context in which it emerged, including the sacred texts (like the Yoga Sutras, Bhagavad Gita, and Hatha Yoga Pradipika), and recognizing the impact of colonialism on the transmission and transformation of these teachings. Practitioners, educators, and institutions must uplift the voices of South Asian teachers, scholars, and communities whose lived experience and ancestral wisdom continue to shape the practice. Acknowledgment also means recognizing how modern yoga—especially in Western wellness industries—has been largely shaped by whiteness, capitalism, and cultural distortion.

Appreciation is a dynamic and relational practice. It involves engaging with yoga through a lens of humility, reciprocity, and care. This may look like naming the South Asian roots of yoga in classes and workshops, compensating lineage holders and educators for their labor, and resisting the commodification of sacred practices. It also includes unlearning the Western emphasis on individualism and performance in favor of yoga's deeper invitation: to live ethically, relationally, and in right alignment with the world. By approaching yoga as a cultural and spiritual inheritance, not a product, we move closer to healing the harm of appropriation and closer to collective liberation. This work is not about perfection, but about intention and integrity, a commitment to remembering, respecting, and restoring what has been fragmented.

1.1.6 What is Trauma-Informed, Mindfulness-Based Yoga?

For those with a history of trauma or incarceration, yoga can provide a trauma-informed, empowering path to healing, fostering self-trust, agency, and reconnection with the body. Accessible and adaptable, yoga and mindfulness are powerful, low-cost tools to enhance longevity, quality of life, and overall well-being, particularly for marginalized populations with limited access to traditional healthcare. Trauma-informed mindfulness-based yoga (TIMBY) is a holistic approach that integrates gentle movement, breathwork, and meditation with an awareness of the impact of trauma on the body and mind. Unlike conventional yoga as taught in the West, TIMBY prioritizes safety, choice, and self-regulation, making it particularly well-suited for aging individuals with a history of incarceration, many of whom have experienced chronic stress, systemic oppression, and adverse childhood experiences. By focusing on interoception (awareness of internal sensations), non-coercive guidance, and adaptability, TIMBY can help formerly incarcerated older adults rebuild trust in their bodies, cultivate self-compassion, and develop stress resilience without triggering past trauma. Furthermore, mindfulness-based practices support nervous system regulation, improving sleep, reducing anxiety and depression, and enhancing overall well-being [31–34]. Given the disproportionate rates of chronic illness, mental health challenges, and social isolation among aging justice-impacted populations, TIMBY offers a culturally responsive, accessible, and low-cost intervention that fosters both physical and emotional healing while promoting agency, empowerment, and community reconnection.

1.1.7 Restorative and Transformative Justice

Restorative justice is a practice rooted in Indigenous wisdom that seeks to repair harm by centering the needs of those most impacted. Rather than punishing the person who caused harm, restorative justice creates space for accountability, dialogue, and mutual understanding. It asks: Who was harmed? What do they need? And who is responsible for meeting those needs? In carceral systems, this approach shifts focus from retribution to reconciliation, offering a more holistic and humane pathway toward justice. Circles, storytelling, and facilitated conversations become vehicles for repair, affirming our shared humanity.

Transformative justice extends this framework by not only addressing harm between individuals but also interrogating and reshaping the systems that give rise to harm in the first place. Transformative justice recognizes that violence is often a symptom of structural oppression—racism, poverty, misogyny, ableism, and more. It asks us to dismantle the conditions that normalize harm while building new systems rooted in equity, dignity, and collective care. This model holds space for accountability while refusing to replicate the logics of punishment and exclusion. It insists that healing and justice must be interconnected and community based.

Healing justice, a term coined by Black and Brown organizers, particularly in the South, centers the necessity of collective healing in movements for liberation. It acknowledges that systems of oppression inflict trauma on individuals and communities, and that sustainable social change must attend to both trauma and transformation. This is where trauma-informed yoga becomes a powerful tool. Trauma-informed yoga honors the body as a site of memory, agency, and restoration. It offers practices that regulate the nervous system, restore a sense of safety, and rebuild the inner connection often fractured by trauma. By weaving together breath, movement, stillness, and choice, trauma-informed yoga invites participants to reclaim sovereignty over their bodies and stories. In spaces of incarceration or reentry, these embodied practices do more than reduce stress—they become acts of resistance, remembrance, and reparation.

1.1.8 Antithesis in Practice and Environment

The contrast between yoga in the contemporary West and in prisons could not be more striking. In studios, yoga is often practiced in solitude, an individual journey toward self-improvement. In prisons, yoga is a communal experience, a rare opportunity for collective healing in an environment where isolation is a primary form of punishment. In the corporate world, yoga is offered as a tool to enhance productivity and work-life balance; in prison, it is a tool to survive the mental and emotional toll of incarceration.

In mainstream Western yoga culture, emphasis is placed on achieving the perfect pose, wearing the right clothing, and mastering increasingly complex postures. In prison, yoga practice encourages one's focus on breath, presence, and simply making it through another day with a modicum of peace. While Western yoga often thrives on consumerism, prison yoga operates on scarcity, where every movement and every breath are a testament to resilience in the face of systemic oppression.

Systemic oppression in carceral settings manifests the constant erosion of personal agency. Incarcerated individuals are often stripped of choice, where to go, when to speak, what to eat, how to move their bodies, within institutions designed to control rather than to heal. This loss of autonomy is compounded by histories of racial, economic, and social injustice that disproportionately funnel Black, Brown, and poor communities into systems of punishment. Within this context, the body itself can become a site of trauma, tension, and hypervigilance, policed from the outside and disconnected from within.

Trauma-informed yoga in prisons disrupts this reality by reintroducing choice, presence, and personal power into the lived experience of participants. In contrast to the dominance and discipline embedded in most aspects of carceral life, yoga offers an invitation: to feel, to choose, to pause, to move—or not. Facilitators trained in trauma-informed approaches emphasize consent, non-coercion, and self-inquiry, encouraging each practitioner to explore their body and breath in a way that feels safe and authentic. This seemingly simple act, deciding how to move or when to rest, can be profoundly liberating in an environment that offers so few opportunities for self-determination. Over time, participants may begin to experience themselves not only as incarcerated, but as embodied, capable, and deeply human.

In this way, yoga becomes more than a practice—it becomes a reclamation of autonomy in the face of systemic control. It offers a space, however small, where participants can practice freedom from within, restore their relationship to their bodies, and reimagine what healing and power feel like on their own terms. It allows individuals to reclaim their breath, their movement, their presence, even if just for an hour. This act of reclaiming oneself, in a system built to erase identity, makes yoga in prisons revolutionary.

1.1.9 The Power of Yoga in Confinement

Despite these stark differences, yoga's transformative potential remains constant. Whether practiced in a sleek studio or a crowded prison cell, yoga offers the possibility of healing, empowerment, and a sense of inner freedom. However, the disparity in access and perception between these two worlds highlights broader systemic inequities. In the West, yoga is often viewed as a luxury, while in prisons, it is sometimes dismissed as an undeserved privilege. Yet, for those behind bars, yoga is not a luxury—it is a lifeline.

By examining yoga's role in these two vastly different contexts, we are forced to ask deeper questions about justice, healing, and who is deemed worthy of care. The presence of yoga in prisons challenges the punitive nature of the carceral system, offering a glimpse of what rehabilitation could look like if intrapersonal and community healing, rather than punishment, were the goal. In this contrast, yoga's true power is revealed—not as a commodity, but as a profound tool for transformation, particularly in the places where it is needed most.

This book examines the profound impact of trauma-informed, mindfulness-based yoga programs in correctional settings, providing a compelling analysis of how yoga serves as a tool for emotional regulation, personal transformation, and resilience among incarcerated individuals. The book juxtaposes yoga's widespread popularity in the contemporary West—where it is often commercialized and commodified—against its potentially radical, revolutionary and rehabilitative role within the prison system. Through research, case studies, and theoretical insights, it presents yoga as more than a wellness practice; it is a means of reclaiming agency, identity, and humanity within spaces of confinement.

1.1.10 Who Will Find This Book Helpful?

This book is a valuable resource for a wide range of readers, including:

- Yoga Teachers & Trauma-Informed Practitioners—Those interested in bringing yoga into underserved and high-trauma populations, particularly within the prison system.
- Criminal Justice Reform Advocates—Individuals working in policy, activism, or non-profit sectors who seek alternative, rehabilitative approaches to incarceration.
- Psychologists, Social Workers & Mental Health Professionals—Practitioners looking to understand the role of somatic practices in addressing trauma and emotional dysregulation in incarcerated populations.
- Educators & Academics—Researchers in fields like sociology, criminology, psychology, and public health who want to explore the intersection of yoga, trauma, and the prison-industrial complex.
- Correctional Facility Administrators & Staff—Those involved in prison programming who are curious about the benefits of yoga for institutional behavior, rehabilitation, and reducing recidivism.
- Anyone Interested in the Intersection of Yoga and Social Justice—Readers passionate about yoga beyond its mainstream representation, seeking to understand its deeper potential for healing and transformation in marginalized communities.

This book challenges conventional narratives about incarceration and rehabilitation, presenting a thought-provoking and evidence-based argument for the expansion of trauma-informed yoga programs in correctional settings. It is a must-read for those who believe in the power of embodiment, mindfulness, and healing, even in the most restrictive environments.

Qualitative research is a method of understanding human and social behavior that emphasizes collecting complex and rich data. In cultivating a profound connection to the body, mind, and heart in compassionate, intuitive, and well-informed ways, individual growth and collective healing are possible and ensured for the study's participants. As an African American woman with family members impacted by incarceration, my lived experiences profoundly shape my approach to research. I recognize that my background informs my commitment to examining systemic inequities and provides a unique lens through which I understand the challenges marginalized communities face. At the same time, I acknowledge the privileges I have been afforded, which have enabled me to pursue academic inquiry and contribute to broader conversations about social justice. This dual awareness drives my commitment to reflexivity—continually interrogating my biases, power dynamics, and assumptions throughout every stage of the research process. I strive to ensure that my work is ethical, inclusive, and sensitive to the nuanced realities of those whose voices are often marginalized while being transparent about how my positionality influences my interpretation of data and overall research outcomes.

1.2 Cradle to Incarceration Pipeline: The Pathway Set Before Birth

For many incarcerated individuals, the road to prison was not a sudden detour but a predetermined path laid long before they were born [19, 22, 35–38]. The concept of the "cradle to incarceration pipeline" suggests that systemic conditions—intergenerational trauma, interpersonal violence, structural racism, and economic inequality—create a cycle of incarceration that is passed from one generation to the next [39–41]. This chapter explores how the seeds of incarceration are planted in early childhood, often before birth, and how trauma, social inequities, and structural violence conspire to make imprisonment not an accident, but an almost inevitable outcome for many individuals of marginalized communities.

1.2.1 Before Birth: The Womb as a Site of Trauma

The journey toward incarceration often begins in the womb. Research has shown that maternal stress, malnutrition, exposure to domestic violence, and substance use during pregnancy can have lasting neurological and psychological effects on a child [42–45]. The prenatal environment, shaped by poverty, racism, and trauma, influences fetal development in ways that increase vulnerability to emotional dysregulation, impulsivity, and behavioral challenges later in life—factors that are strongly correlated with incarceration.

Intergenerational trauma, the transmission of psychological wounds across generations, means that many incarcerated individuals were born to parents who themselves suffered significant adversity. A mother who was abused as a child, who grew up in a neighborhood plagued by gun violence, or who experienced chronic stress from racial discrimination carries those traumas in her body. These experiences shape fetal brain development, particularly in the regions responsible for stress regulation, emotional control, and impulse management. The epigenetic effects of trauma—where stress and hardship alter gene expression—suggest that the effects of racialized poverty, mass incarceration, and systemic violence are imprinted at a cellular level, making some children biologically predisposed to heightened stress responses.

For Black and Indigenous mothers, the risks are even greater [46–49]. Black maternal mortality rates in the U.S. are alarmingly high, driven by systemic medical neglect, chronic stress, and racism in healthcare. Pregnant women who experience racism and poverty are more likely to give birth to premature, low-birth-weight infants, increasing the child's likelihood of developmental and behavioral problems. In this way, the system fails individuals before they even take their first breath, reinforcing the generational cycle of disadvantage that leads to higher rates of incarceration [35, 41, 50, 51].

1.3 The Wounds That Never Heal: Maternal and Paternal Abuse and Neglect

The home is often the first battleground in the cradle-to-incarceration pipeline. Many incarcerated individuals were born into environments of chronic instability, where basic needs were unmet, and violence—whether emotional, physical, or structural—was part of daily life.

Neglect, abuse, and toxic stress are key predictors of future incarceration. The landmark Adverse Childhood Experiences (ACEs) study found that children exposed to chronic stressors such as parental substance abuse, domestic violence, or neglect are exponentially more likely to develop mental health issues, engage in criminalized behaviors, and become involved in the juvenile justice system [38, 52, 53]. When a child's home is not a place of safety but a source of trauma, their nervous system is wired for survival rather than stability.

- Children who grow up witnessing domestic violence often develop heightened stress responses, making them more prone to aggression or hypervigilance—traits that can lead to disciplinary issues in school and early criminalization [9, 50, 51].
- Children in households affected by substance abuse often experience neglect, housing instability, and food insecurity, all of which disrupt normal childhood development and increase vulnerability to delinquency [54–57].
- Children of incarcerated parents face profound emotional and psychological challenges. With an estimated 2.7 million children in the U.S. having an incarcerated parent, these children are six times more likely to be incarcerated themselves [36, 58–60].

The school system, rather than serving as an intervention point, too often reinforces the trajectory toward incarceration. The school-to-prison pipeline, a well-documented phenomenon, disproportionately affects Black, Latino, and Indigenous children, who are far more likely to be suspended, expelled, or referred to law enforcement for disciplinary issues than their white peers [61–63]. Zero-tolerance policies, the criminalization of normal childhood behavior, and the over-policing of marginalized communities funnel children directly from classrooms to jail cells.

A Black kindergartener who throws a tantrum may be handcuffed rather than comforted. A teenager who struggles with emotional regulation due to early trauma may be labeled a "problem child" rather than receiving mental health support. A child struggling in poverty may act out in class due to hunger or neglect but is met with punishment rather than compassion. When schools become extensions of the carceral system, rather than sanctuaries of learning and growth, they accelerate the cycle of incarceration.

1.3.1 Structural Violence and the Path to Incarceration

Even beyond the home and school, the broader structural conditions of American society ensure that certain communities are disproportionately targeted for incarceration. Structural violence—the systemic, institutionalized ways that harm is inflicted on marginalized groups—plays a central role in the cradle-to-incarceration pipeline [64–66]. Poverty is one of the strongest predictors of incarceration. In many communities, economic opportunities are intentionally limited due to policies like redlining, job discrimination, and underfunded public services [67–70]. When legal avenues for survival are scarce, individuals—especially young men—turn to informal economies (e.g., drug trade, underground labor) to support themselves and their families. These survival strategies are then criminalized, further entrenching individuals in the justice system.

Housing instability also plays a significant role. Children who grow up in environments where eviction, homelessness, or unsafe housing are common are more likely to enter the foster care system—a direct pipeline to incarceration [56, 71, 72]. An overwhelming number of incarcerated individuals spent time in foster care, where neglect and abuse are rampant, and criminalization is high.

1.3.2 Racialized Policing and Over-Criminalization

From an early age, Black and Brown children—especially boys—are seen as threats rather than as vulnerable youth in need of support [73–78]. Studies show that Black boys as young as 5 years old are perceived as older and less innocent than their white peers. This racial bias translates into disproportionate police encounters, where Black and Latino youth are more likely to be arrested, charged as adults, and receive harsher sentences for the same offenses as white youth.

The War on Drugs, mandatory minimums, and stop-and-frisk policies have all contributed to the mass incarceration of Black and Brown men, creating a cycle where incarceration becomes not just a possibility but an expectation [79–81].

Entire communities have been systematically targeted, ensuring that incarceration is not an individual failing but a collective reality.

1.3.3 Methodology

This book focuses on the experience of formerly incarcerated men who participated in trauma-informed, mindfulness-based yoga classes. Participants from this study were formerly incarcerated at San Quentin State Prison and were recruited via a flyer shared on listservs via email and social media within groups for formerly incarcerated people and prison program providers. The participants were all male and identified as African American, Hispanic, or White. The participants chose pseudonyms to protect their anonymity and then briefly introduced themselves. Additionally, all participants' personally identifiable information (PII) was kept confidential to protect their privacy.

Eight participants enrolled in the study and were interviewed virtually. The interview questions detailed the participants' experiences in the yoga classes, their perceived effects of the classes while incarcerated, and the long-term effects of their participation after release. This inquiry included a somatic depth psychological approach to give space for the body's voice. Some of the questions directly addressed if the yoga practice impacted participants' relationships and, if so, in what ways this result manifested for them. The questions highlighted the body's relationship to mindfulness-based, trauma-informed practices to address the research question effectively.

The integration of phenomenological, anti-oppressive, and somatic depth psychological frameworks was essential to the development of this study's qualitative methodology, precisely because of the immense, layered challenges inherent to carceral settings. Traditional research approaches often risk flattening or abstracting the lived experiences of incarcerated individuals, especially when they are filtered through institutional or deficit-based lenses. A phenomenological approach, by contrast, centers the subjective, first-person accounts of participants, treating their embodied narratives as sites of knowledge rather than pathology. This allowed the study to attend not only to what participants said, but to how they experienced healing through breath, movement, and presence—honoring the depth and dignity of their inner lives.

An anti-oppressive lens further ensured that the research design actively resisted reproducing the hierarchies and power imbalances that participants already endure in carceral systems. This involved cultivating reciprocal, respectful relationships, creating space for participant voice and agency, and acknowledging the broader structural forces—such as racism, poverty, and punishment—that shape the context of incarceration. By embedding somatic depth psychology into the methodology, the study also validated the body as a site of meaning-making, trauma, and transformation. It recognized that healing is not just a cognitive process, but a deeply felt, bodily one—often occurring below the surface of language. Together, these frameworks enabled a methodology that was not only rigorous, but also ethically attuned, relationally grounded, and spacious enough to hold the complexity, pain, and possibility that arise when studying healing in systems designed to harm.

While the challenges within carceral settings are immense and multifaceted, the exploration of effective interventions remains critical. Yoga, as a holistic practice, offers a unique pathway toward healing, rehabilitation, and resilience for incarcerated individuals. To further illuminate its impact and applicability, this book will share the stories of yoga participants and present the results of a qualitative study that delves into their lived experiences. The participants' descriptive characteristics can be found in Fig. 1.1. By weaving together personal narratives with empirical findings, this work aims to provide a comprehensive and nuanced understanding of how yoga can serve as a meaningful tool for personal transformation and well-being within the confines of prison life.

Each participant provided a brief introduction in their own words that included their unique perceptions of their yoga practice. The purpose was to provide additional insight into each individual and shed light on the transferability of the findings.

1.3.4 Participant Biographies

1.3.4.1 Jack

My name is Jack, and I am 43 years old. I have a 15-year-old son, and I live in Santa Maria. I work as a maintenance technician at a country club in Santa Barbara County. I learned about the yoga program from watching a video in the media center while incarcerated at San Quentin state prison. The lady in the video was teaching a group of students about yoga and easily holding challenging positions. I was inspired to try yoga. One of my most memorable moments in yoga was when we all attempted to do a position where we rested on our shoulders while our feet were straight up in the air. We all used the wall to keep us erect, and to the best of our knowledge, we were completing the pose until the instructor calmly called out, "I see a bunch of bananas out there"! There was a collective gasp of laughter, and most of us crumpled to the floor!

Fig. 1.1 Participants' Characteristics

Men	n = 8
Average Age	46
Race/ Ethnicity	
• Black/ African American	2
• Hispanic	2
• White	4
Average length of incarceration	23 years
Average time since release	2.7 years

1.3.4.2 Leroy

My name is Leroy, and I am 58 years old. I was first introduced to the practice of yoga by a friend at San Quentin, where I was paroled in 2022. I always thought that yoga was for hippies, plus it looked so easy. That perception quickly changed after my first yoga class at San Quentin in 2018. I stretched muscles I didn't know even existed. Although my body was sore, it wasn't a painful soreness. It was a mentally rewarding experience for me. Then Covid-19 hit, essentially shutting everything down in San Quentin. I was at a loss at being unable to practice yoga. However, as soon as I was paroled, I found a new yoga community in San Luis Obispo and continued my yoga practice. However, a significant difference existed between a prison yoga setting and the yoga studio in San Luis Obispo. Nevertheless, I discovered similarities between breathing and effortless effort no matter what setting was.

1.3.4.3 Derek

While incarcerated at San Quentin, I heard much about the yoga program from friends who took the classes. They got me interested in it by talking positively about the program, and eventually, I was curious enough to try it. That was 8 years ago, and now I practice yoga on and off. My most memorable yoga moment is lying on my mat staring up at the ceiling during savasana. In those moments, I could reflect and find peace never present in prison. I continue to use breathing practices throughout my day to help with stress, focus, and concentration.

1.3.4.4 Wade

My name is Wade, and I am 53 years old. I served 29 years in prison; I was released in 2018. I am a full-time student pursuing a degree in economics and work part-time building custom crates for freight shipping. My yoga practice is a vital part of my self-care. I was at Soledad prison in 2010 when a friend at San Quentin started taking yoga classes. He told me about it and had the organziation send me a book about yoga. I tried to practice, but it wasn't until I transferred to San Quentin in 2012 and started to take yoga classes that I began to develop a practice.

1.3.4.5 Jake

As soon as I arrived at San Quentin each unit, I began to hear from others, including Ron Self, the lead incarcerated facilitator and creator of Veterans Healing Veterans from the Inside Out, about yoga as one of the programs offered. Before my incarceration, yoga had always interested me, but it had never been a part of my life; it had always been just out of reach, as economic or time constraints prevented it. Now I could join a class as I had both the time and the means as it (the classes) was free.

My practice began at San Quentin in mid-2014. I took classes twice a week; one class in H-unit on Fridays and one with the veterans' group earlier in the week. I continued my practice to this day, finding opportunities throughout each day to incorporate an asana or two as time permits.

1.3.4.6 Andre

I spent 23 years in prison. I started taking yoga classes in 2011 until I got out in 2020. The classes transformed me. Now that I am out, I am doing everything I can to give back what was given to me. I am trying to help the brothers and sisters stay out of prison. I am trying to help the youth. I organized a backpack drive for the start of the school year and trips for the kids in the neighborhood. I run several businesses too. It's by the grace of God that God put people in my life that can show me how not to give up. With all that in mind, I can't let everyone down. I wake up at 4:30 every morning and begin my practice to help me get through the day.

1.3.4.7 Manuel

My name is Manuel; I am 50 years old and a native of Perú. I spent 23 years incarcerated in the California Correctional System. I was blessed to have spent the last 9 years at San Quentin State Prison (S.Q.). I said "blessed" because it was not until this time that I finally felt hope and realized that perhaps going home was a possibility. San Quentin was like no other prison I had ever experienced. It offered a variety of self-help groups that helped me grow and become a better human being. Among the many programs, there was the yoga classes, which to no surprise, had a 1.5–2-year waiting list. It was around 2012 that I finally joined the Tuesday class, and excitement and optimism initiated my journey.

1.3.4.8 Ernesto

I first found out about the yoga program through my running partner. He had put me on the list, and a week later, I met the yoga teacher. I practiced yoga for about 5 years. I wish I had been introduced to the practice sooner. I felt this way shortly after my first practice. My favorite aspect of my yoga practice is that it allows me to check out of my external life and check in with my internal state of being. I practice yoga daily through conscious breathing, listening to my body, and applying mindfulness to my hobbies, such as art and photography.

1.4 Assessment of Traumatic States of Incarcerated Populations

Yoga and mindfulness, when integrated into trauma-informed interventions, can serve as powerful tools for breaking cycles of intergenerational trauma and incarceration. Programs that teach self-regulation, resilience, and emotional processing have the potential to intervene before young people enter the prison system. If incarceration begins in the womb, then healing must begin there, too. By shifting from a system of punishment to a system of prevention and care, we can begin to dismantle the cradle-to-incarceration pipeline and replace it with pathways toward healing, stability, and liberation. The integration of yoga and mindfulness into trauma-informed interventions offers a compassionate, holistic approach that acknowledges the interconnectedness of body, mind, and spirit. By fostering emotional resilience, self-regulation, and a deeper sense of self-awareness, these practices provide a foundation upon which healing and transformation can occur, even in the most challenging environments. As we continue to listen to the voices of those directly impacted, their stories challenge us to reimagine a system that prioritizes care, compassion, and restoration over punishment. In doing so, we not only support those currently incarcerated but also contribute to breaking cycles of trauma and incarceration for generations to come.

Chapter 2
The Dysregulated Body: Trauma, Protection, and Connection in Yoga for Incarcerated Populations

The human body is not merely a biological organism; it is an archive of lived experience, a repository of every joy, wound, and survival mechanism accumulated over time. Nowhere is this more evident than in the bodies of those who have endured trauma—particularly those who find themselves incarcerated, carrying histories of violence, neglect, and systemic oppression. The concept of dysregulation is central to understanding trauma's impact on the nervous system and behavior. Dysregulation can manifest in emotional volatility, chronic stress, dissociation, impulsivity, and difficulty with relationships—all of which are overrepresented in incarcerated populations.

In the carceral system, dysregulation is often treated as a behavioral issue rather than a symptom of trauma. Instead of support, individuals experience punishment, isolation, and further deprivation, reinforcing cycles of harm. The prison system was not built to heal; it was built to contain. However, trauma-informed approaches—particularly through yoga—offer a powerful means of addressing dysregulation at its root, reconnecting individuals to their bodies, emotions, and capacity for self-regulation. Jake, a participant in the yoga program, explained, "4 years of practice at San Quentin, one of the things that the facilitator impressed upon us is that we can practice yoga at any time and any place in the space with or without prompts." To understand why trauma-informed yoga is essential for incarcerated populations, we must first examine the role of protection and connection in early childhood development, the relational foundation necessary for emotional regulation, and the ways in which co-regulation can become a path to healing—even in the most restrictive environments.

C. Williams, *Yoga in Prisons*, SpringerBriefs in Offending Populations & Correctional Psychotherapy, https://doi.org/10.1007/978-3-031-98368-9_2

2.1 Protection and Connection: The Foundations of Nervous System Regulation

From the moment of birth, an infant's nervous system depends entirely on the responsiveness of caregivers to develop a sense of safety in the world [82–84]. Secure attachment in early childhood lays the foundation for emotional resilience, self-regulation, and the ability to engage in healthy relationships. When a child experiences consistent protection and connection, their nervous system learns to oscillate fluidly between states of alertness and calm, between effort and rest, between activation and recovery.

But what happens when protection is absent? When caregivers are abusive, neglectful, or emotionally unavailable, the child's nervous system adapts to an unpredictable world. This adaptation often takes the form of chronic dysregulation—heightened reactivity, difficulty calming down, and a deep-seated distrust of others [85–89]. Instead of learning that relationships are a source of safety, they become sources of fear. The body internalizes this reality, remaining in a constant state of hypervigilance or dissociation.

Andre experienced a particularly challenging time after his parole date was revoked; he explained: "If that (having his parole date revoked) would have happened before I went to yoga, I would have copped out, but due to yoga, I was able to breathe. I was able to stay centered and stay focused on the prize, and what I valued was going home to be with my family." In this way, trauma-informed yoga is not about performance; it is about **reclaiming a sense of inner control**. It is about recognizing that, despite external confinement, there is still space within the body where freedom can exist.

For many incarcerated individuals, childhood was not a place of safety but a battleground [19, 20, 35, 39, 59]. Research consistently shows high rates of adverse childhood experiences (ACEs) among incarcerated populations, including exposure to violence, parental incarceration, substance abuse, and physical or sexual abuse. These early disruptions to protection and connection shape the nervous system in ways that persist into adulthood, often manifesting as impulsivity, aggression, addiction, or emotional shutdown—coping mechanisms for a world that has never felt safe. In the absence of protective relationships, the nervous system remains stuck in survival mode. This is where trauma-informed yoga becomes essential. It provides a structured, embodied way to rebuild a sense of safety, offering the possibility of connection—not just with others, but with oneself.

Andre grew up in a neighborhood marked by poverty, violence, and instability. Born to a teenage mother and an absent father, his early childhood was spent moving between the cramped apartments of various relatives. The adults in his life were often consumed by their own struggles—addiction, financial hardship, and cycles of trauma that spanned generations. Despite the chaos surrounding him, Andre was a bright, curious child who craved stability and connection. Yet, the absence of consistent nurturing and guidance left him vulnerable to the harsh realities of his environment. By the time he reached adolescence, Andre had already witnessed more violence than many experience in a lifetime, and the trauma of his upbringing cast a long shadow over his sense of self and possibility.

2.1.1 *Breaking the Cycle: The Role of Healing and Intervention*

If the pathway to incarceration is set before birth, then intervention must also begin early. Healing the cradle-to-incarceration pipeline requires addressing the root causes: trauma, poverty, structural violence, and systemic racism. This means:

- Expanding trauma-informed education and social services to support children from high-risk backgrounds before they enter the criminal justice system.
- Investing in community-based mental health programs that address the long-term effects of childhood trauma and adverse experiences.
- Reforming punitive school policies that criminalize Black and Brown children and replacing them with restorative justice models.
- Challenging systemic economic inequalities by providing job training, housing support, and fair wages to break cycles of poverty.

2.1.2 *Relating and Regulation: Trauma-Informed Yoga as a Path to Self-Healing*

At its core, yoga is a practice of self-regulation and learning to work with the breath, movement, and stillness to cultivate inner steadiness. For those who have experienced trauma, however, self-regulation is not automatic—it must be learned. Before the nervous system can regulate itself, it must first experience co-regulation—the presence of a safe, attuned other who helps stabilize and soothe [86, 88].

Traditional yoga classes often focus on posture alignment and physical endurance, but trauma-informed yoga prioritizes the felt sense of safety [30, 90–92]. The instructor's role is not to impose rigid sequences but to offer choice, autonomy, and an atmosphere of non-judgment. This approach recognizes that for many incarcerated individuals, their bodies have been sites of harm, punishment, and control. Rather than forcing a particular posture, trauma-informed yoga invites practitioners to explore movement in ways that feel safe and accessible. This process is deeply relational. Even in a prison setting—where autonomy is systematically stripped away—yoga can become a rare space of permission. Participants are encouraged to notice their breath, sense their body, and make choices about how they move. Over time, these small acts of self-awareness contribute to a shift in the nervous system: from hypervigilance to groundedness, from dissociation to presence.

Breathing practices are particularly powerful in this regard. For someone who has lived in a state of survival for years, shallow, rapid breathing may become the default state. Learning to slow and deepen the breath signals to the nervous system that it is safe to relax. These practices are not just theoretical; they are physiological tools that help rewire the stress response [11–14, 93]. In this way, trauma-informed yoga is not about performance; it is about reclaiming a sense of inner control. It is about recognizing that, despite external confinement, there is still space within the body where freedom can exist.

2.2 What Does a Trauma-Informed, Mindfulness-Based Yoga Class Look Like?

2.2.1 *Co-Regulation: Healing in Community*

While self-regulation is the goal, co-regulation is the bridge that makes it possible. Co-regulation occurs when a regulated nervous system helps stabilize a dysregulated one. This is why an infant calms when held by a caregiver and why a distressed person finds relief in the presence of a compassionate friend. For many incarcerated individuals, relationships have been fraught with instability, conflict, or harm. Trust is not easily given, and for good reason. Yet, human healing does not happen in isolation—it happens in relationship. Trauma-informed yoga programs in prisons create a unique opportunity for co-regulation to take place, even in an environment designed to sever connection. The presence of a compassionate facilitator—a teacher who embodies steadiness and care—offers a model of safety. Even without direct physical contact, a calm voice, consistent presence, and attuned energy can have a profound impact.

Beyond the practice itself, co-regulation extends into how participants engage with one another. Many who have completed trauma-informed yoga programs in prison go on to teach or guide others, creating a ripple effect of healing. This sense of responsibility and shared experience transforms yoga from an individual practice into a communal one, reinforcing the idea that healing is not just personal—it is collective.

Chapter 3
The Healing Nature of an Ethical Relationship

The relationship between a facilitator and incarcerated individuals is the cornerstone of any successful trauma-informed yoga practice. This relationship, however, goes beyond the simple transmission of yoga techniques or practices; it is about cultivating trust, respect, and emotional safety in an environment marked by distrust, dehumanization, and chronic trauma. The very foundation of trauma-informed yoga rests on the belief that the healing process begins with the relationship—the dynamic between the facilitator and the participant. In the context of prisons, where isolation, violence, and institutional control govern every aspect of life, the presence of a compassionate, nonjudgmental facilitator can offer a rare moment of reprieve and genuine care.

Yoga, at its essence, is a practice of reconnecting—connecting to the body, the breath, and the self. However, for those who have endured significant trauma, particularly in correctional facilities, these connections can be elusive. Prison environments are designed to disrupt these natural connections by enforcing strict routines, invasive surveillance, and systemic neglect. For incarcerated individuals, who may have spent years dissociating from their bodies as a means of survival, the introduction of yoga can serve as a counter to these disconnections, offering a space for reclamation and healing. However, to unlock yoga's true potential as a healing tool, the facilitator must embody a role that goes beyond teaching postures: they must be a holder of space, a model of ethical presence, and an advocate for trauma recovery.

3.1 The Facilitator's Role: Holding Space and Building Trust

The yoga facilitator in prison must first understand that their role extends far beyond the transmission of physical poses. Their job is to create an environment that feels safe, empowering, and healing for individuals who have experienced deep trauma. The importance of safety cannot be overstated. The traumatic experiences of many

C. Williams, *Yoga in Prisons*, SpringerBriefs in Offending Populations & Correctional Psychotherapy, https://doi.org/10.1007/978-3-031-98368-9_3

incarcerated individuals—ranging from childhood abuse and neglect to the violence and systemic oppression within the prison system—have left a deep impact on their nervous systems. Trauma rewires the brain and the body, leaving individuals in a heightened state of alertness or dissociation, unable to process emotions or connect with their surroundings [82, 84, 86].

A trauma-informed facilitator understands that every action in the yoga class—every word spoken, every instruction given—must reflect a commitment to safety. In a prison setting, safety can feel elusive; the constant presence of guards, the oppressive atmosphere, and the inherent instability of the environment make it difficult for participants to trust even basic offerings. Thus, the facilitator's first task is to create predictability within the yoga session. Predictability offers a small but crucial sense of control in an environment where control is often out of reach.

The facilitator can build this predictability by maintaining a consistent structure for each class. For example, beginning each session with grounding practices like breath awareness or body scanning allows participants to center themselves before diving into the more physically demanding postures. This stability is essential for participants who have been subjected to erratic and unpredictable environments in prison. Grounding exercises, such as focusing on the feet or feeling the body press into the floor, create a sense of orientation, helping individuals feel more in control of their bodies. For those who have been disconnected from their bodies due to trauma, this grounding can be the first step toward reclaiming a sense of safety.

Importantly, facilitators must approach yoga as an offering rather than a directive. Many incarcerated individuals have experienced harsh authoritarianism and coercion throughout their lives, both in the outside world and within the prison system. A trauma-informed facilitator recognizes the importance of offering choices and empowering participants. In traditional yoga, instructors may dictate the pace or order of poses, but in a trauma-informed class, facilitators offer alternatives: "If this doesn't feel good for you, feel free to modify," or "Take a break anytime you need, sitting comfortably or resting in child's pose (balasana)." This emphasis on autonomy restores a sense of control for participants and fosters a supportive environment where they can engage with the practice on their own terms.

3.1.1 The Ethical Foundation of Yoga: Respecting the Humanity of Each Individual

One of the most profound aspects of trauma-informed yoga in prisons is the ethical relationship that develops between the facilitator and the participants. Prisons are institutions that perpetuate cycles of dehumanization. The very purpose of incarceration—punishment, isolation, and control—creates an environment in which individuals are often reduced to their worst actions. The language of "offenders" or "inmates" serves to strip incarcerated individuals of their dignity and humanity. In such an environment, yoga becomes a radical act of resistance, not only to the prison system but also to the trauma that has shaped the lives of those within it.

A trauma-informed facilitator must embody a philosophy that honors and respects the humanity of every individual, regardless of their past or present circumstances [98]. This means shifting away from judgmental labels and instead seeing the person beyond the crime. Incarcerated individuals, often treated as disposable by society, may have internalized these labels, leading to feelings of shame, guilt, and worthlessness. The facilitator, through ethical presence, can counteract these feelings by treating each participant with the utmost respect. They are not seen as criminals, but as individuals seeking healing, growth, and connection.

This ethical relationship also involves acknowledging the power imbalance that exists between the facilitator and the participants. While the facilitator may hold authority in guiding the yoga practice, their role is not to impose their expertise or agenda. Instead, they must create an environment of mutual respect, where the participants' autonomy balances the facilitator's power. This power dynamic is particularly significant in prison settings, where authority figures frequently demand compliance and exert control. Yoga is not about submission; it is about connection, self-awareness, and freedom. The facilitator's role, then, is not to correct or change the participants but to offer a space where they can reconnect with themselves on their own terms.

3.2 Respect Begins Within: Foundational Teachings in Yoga

3.2.1 Facilitating Emotional Healing: Working with Trauma Responses

Many incarcerated individuals have experienced extensive emotional trauma, which can manifest in a variety of ways during yoga practice [20–22]. Trauma responses, such as dissociation, hypervigilance, or emotional numbing, can make it difficult for participants to stay present or engage in the practice. A trauma-informed facilitator is attuned to these responses and works gently to help participants re-establish a connection with their bodies and emotions.

This approach requires a deep understanding of the physiological impact of trauma. Trauma often leads to dysregulation of the autonomic nervous system, which controls bodily functions such as heart rate, digestion, and breathing. Individuals who have experienced trauma may feel constantly on edge or may have difficulty relaxing, even in seemingly safe environments. In yoga, this may manifest as difficulty with deep breathing, tension in the body, or an inability to remain still.

Facilitators can address these responses by offering grounding techniques and encouraging self-awareness. For example, facilitators may guide participants to focus on their breath or to notice sensations in their hands or feet, helping them reconnect with the present moment and calm their nervous system. These grounding techniques are not only effective in helping participants manage trauma responses but also in teaching them to regulate their emotions and re-establish their body's sense of equilibrium.

In some cases, emotional responses may emerge during yoga practice—tears, anger, frustration, or sadness. Facilitators must be prepared to navigate these emotions with compassion and care. In a trauma-informed class, participants are not judged for their emotional expressions but are supported as they process and release pent-up feelings. The facilitator's role is to hold space for these emotions without rushing them, allowing participants to feel safe in expressing their vulnerabilities.

3.2.2 Transformative Potential of the Ethical Relationship

The power of an ethical, trauma-informed relationship is transformative. For many incarcerated individuals, yoga offers the first opportunity to reconnect with their bodies, their emotions, and their sense of self-worth. By building trust, offering choices, and respecting autonomy, the facilitator helps participants reclaim a sense of agency that has often been stripped away by years of trauma and institutional control.

The long-term impact of these relationships can be profound. Yoga participants in prison often report feeling a greater sense of control over their emotions and their reactions, which in turn can improve their behavior and relationships within the prison system. Some individuals, empowered by their experience with yoga, go on to become yoga teachers themselves, sharing the practice with their peers and continuing the cycle of healing and empowerment. Jack shared how this practice taught him how to perceive the world more skillfully than he did before incarceration; he stated, "I became receptive to human kindness, softness. I started understanding that just because the person said something or looked at me wrong doesn't mean that that was aimed at me, right? And then I learned the most valuable piece of it all. Allow it to come and go from your mind, and it does." Jack's reflection illustrates the transformative impact of a healing, ethical relationship with the yoga facilitator. His growing receptivity to human kindness and his ability to pause before reacting signal more than internal change—they point to the presence of a consistent, compassionate presence in the yoga space. This relationship likely modeled emotional safety, nonjudgment, and attuned care, allowing Jack to experience a sense of trust and connection that may have been rare or absent in his life prior to incarceration. The facilitator's ethical stance—grounded in humility, respect, and relational integrity—created the conditions for Jack to soften, to question old narratives, and to access the liberating insight that thoughts and emotions can rise and fall without overtaking him. In this way, the facilitator did not just guide a practice, but held a space where healing became possible.

The facilitator's role, while essential in the moment, also contributes to a larger movement within the prison system—one that seeks to humanize incarcerated individuals, promote rehabilitation, and offer tools for emotional and psychological healing. By fostering ethical relationships rooted in respect and compassion, the facilitator plays a critical role in breaking the cycle of trauma and empowering incarcerated individuals to heal and grow. Through yoga, they show that healing is not only possible but also a fundamental right, even in the most restrictive environments.

3.2.3 *Breaking the Cycle: The Long-Term Impact of Ethical Facilitation*

When trauma-informed yoga is introduced in correctional facilities, it plants the seed of something revolutionary: the idea that healing is possible even within the confines of incarceration. The ethical relationship between facilitator and participant is the foundation upon which this healing is built, and its impact extends far beyond the walls of the yoga class. It has the potential to shift an individual's self-perception, alter institutional dynamics, and even challenge the punitive framework of the prison system itself.

Many incarcerated individuals enter the carceral system with deeply ingrained narratives of unworthiness, guilt, and disconnection from their own humanity [20, 90–92, 99, 100]. These narratives are often reinforced by a lifetime of systemic oppression, abuse, neglect, and, ultimately, the prison system itself. A trauma-informed facilitator works to disrupt these narratives—not through force or coercion, but by consistently showing up with respect, presence, and an unwavering belief in the dignity of every person in the room.

This approach is powerful because it is so different from what many incarcerated individuals have experienced in their interactions with authority figures. Correctional officers, legal professionals, and even some mental health practitioners often operate within the framework of control and compliance. In contrast, the trauma-informed yoga facilitator offers something rare: a relationship that is nonjudgmental, collaborative, and rooted in choice. Over time, this consistency can help participants shift from a mindset of survival to one of self-inquiry and healing.

For those who engage with yoga on a regular basis, the long-term benefits become clear. Studies have shown that trauma-informed yoga in prison reduces symptoms of PTSD, anxiety, and depression [11–15, 90]. It improves self-regulation, emotional resilience, and even physical health outcomes. But beyond these measurable benefits, something more intangible but equally profound occurs participants begin to reclaim their sense of self.

3.2.4 Acknowledging the Role of Race, Gender, Sexual Orientation and Difference in the Healing Relationship

This work would be incomplete if it did not discuss the role of diversity in the healing relationship. In healing relationships—particularly within trauma-informed yoga, psychotherapy, or holistic health care—positionality refers to the social and political context that shapes a practitioner's identity, including race, gender, class, sexual orientation, ability, and cultural background. These intersecting identities influence how one is perceived, how one perceives others, and how power is negotiated within the therapeutic space [101, 102]. Practitioners aware of their positionality can better navigate the inherent power differentials and create relational dynamics rooted in humility, mutual respect, and embodied ethics.

Racial concordance, or shared racial or ethnic identity between provider and participant, has fostered greater trust, communication, and perceived empathy [103, 104]. For people with histories of racialized trauma, such as chronic exposure to racism, state violence, incarceration, and systemic marginalization, racial concordance can create a felt sense of safety and cultural resonance. However, while concordance may facilitate connection, it is not a substitute for deep cultural humility or competency.

Cultural competency, in the context of racialized trauma, must evolve beyond superficial awareness of cultural difference to include a trauma-informed, anti-racist, and intersectional praxis [105, 106]. This consists of the practitioner's willingness to:

- Acknowledge historical and intergenerational trauma rooted in colonization, slavery, incarceration, and systemic violence.
- Recognize their own biases, privileges, and social positioning without defensiveness.
- Practice cultural humility, listening deeply, and honoring the lived experiences of those they serve.
- Embodying a non-dominating presence involves regulating their nervous systems, avoiding reenactments of racialized power, and co-creating spaces of dignity and autonomy [107].

For practitioners working in carceral environments or with populations disproportionately impacted by racial violence, this means integrating both structural awareness and somatic attunement—honoring how trauma lives in the body and how systems, or structures, of oppression compound that trauma. A trauma-informed, racially conscious approach is not merely about avoiding harm but actively contributing to liberatory healing, restoring agency, connection, and a sense of belonging.

While cultural competency focuses on acquiring knowledge about different cultures, and cultural humility emphasizes a lifelong commitment to self-evaluation, mutual respect, and listening across difference, structural competency expands the frame to include the social, political, and economic structures that produce health disparities and trauma [108]. It calls on practitioners to recognize how policies, institutions, and systems, such as mass incarceration, redlining, medical racism, and educational inequity, shape the health and healing outcomes of marginalized communities. Whereas cultural competency can risk essentializing identity, cultural humility centers on interpersonal awareness, and structural competency demands that practitioners see beyond the individual body and toward the body politic, cultivating the ability to identify and intervene in the structural determinants of suffering. In trauma-informed yoga or therapeutic relationships, this means not only attuning to embodied trauma but also understanding how historical and systemic forces—genocide, racism, colonization, gender oppression—continue to live in the nervous system and shape access to safety, rest, and recovery.

In addition to race, healing relationships must be attentive to the intersecting dimensions of gender, sexual orientation, class, ability, religion, body size, immigration status, and other social identities that shape how individuals experience trauma and healing. Drawing from intersectionality theory [102], it becomes clear that people do not experience oppression or care in single-issue terms; instead, they embody layered identities that may intensify vulnerability or invisibility within healing spaces. For instance, a queer woman of color navigating trauma may carry distinct somatic imprints of racialized misogyny and homophobia that are not addressed through generic trauma-informed approaches. Trans and gender-expansive individuals, especially in carceral or institutional settings, often encounter systemic erasure, violence, or misrecognition that compounds their trauma. Therefore, a truly trauma-informed, equity-rooted approach must include intersectional awareness, gender-affirming practices, and anti-oppressive frameworks that validate lived experiences, protect agency, and create conditions for trust and liberation. Without this nuanced attention, the healing relationship risks reinforcing the very systems of domination it seeks to disrupt.

3.2.5 From Disembodiment to Reconnection: The Journey Back to the Self

One of the most damaging effects of trauma is disembodiment—the severing of the connection between mind and body [109–113]. For many incarcerated individuals, this dissociation has been a survival mechanism, a way to endure the unendurable. Whether through substance use, aggression, or emotional numbing, the body has often been treated as an adversary rather than an ally. The ethical presence of a trauma-informed facilitator helps reverse this process [98]. Through movement, breath, and stillness, participants gradually learn to inhabit their bodies again—not as sites of pain or punishment, but as vessels of experience and wisdom. This process can be slow and nonlinear; some days, participants may feel fully engaged, while other days, their trauma responses may make it challenging to stay present. A skilled facilitator recognizes and honors this variability, reinforcing the message that there is no right or wrong way to engage with the practice.

3.3 Becoming a Skilled Facilitator

3.3.1 Self-Inquiry

3.3.1.1 Personal Beliefs: Prison Reform or Revolution

This re-embodiment is not just about physical sensation—it is about reclaiming a sense of agency [88, 114, 15]. In a system that strips individuals of choice, autonomy, and self-determination, yoga offers a rare moment of empowerment. The simple act of choosing how to move, how to breathe, or whether to engage in a particular posture is an assertion of selfhood. Over time, this sense of autonomy can extend beyond the mat, influencing how individuals navigate their relationships, their emotions, and even their path forward upon release.

3.3.2 The Ripple Effect: Changing Institutional Culture

While the primary impact of trauma-informed yoga is on the individual, its effects do not stop there. As incarcerated individuals experience personal transformation, they also influence the culture around them. This ripple effect can be seen in multiple ways. First, the interpersonal relationships within prison communities often shift as participants develop greater emotional regulation and self-awareness. Many incarcerated individuals operate in survival mode, where reactions are driven by fear, anger, or past trauma. Yoga helps cultivate a pause—a moment of awareness before reaction. Over time, this increased emotional regulation can lead to fewer conflicts, stronger peer relationships, and even a sense of collective support within the prison population.

Second, facilitators who consistently show up with respect and integrity can influence the way incarcerated individuals expect to be treated. Many individuals in the carceral system have internalized messages that they are unworthy of kindness or respect. When a facilitator treats them with dignity, it challenges these deeply ingrained beliefs. This shift can have powerful implications, as participants begin to demand and expect more humane treatment from others, including prison staff. In some facilities, correctional officers and prison administrators have begun to recognize the positive impact of yoga on incarcerated individuals, leading to increased institutional support for these programs [115]. While resistance still exists, the growing body of research on the benefits of trauma-informed yoga is making it harder to dismiss. Some correctional institutions have even begun integrating yoga and mindfulness into their official rehabilitation programs, acknowledging its role in reducing recidivism and improving mental health.

3.3.3 Beyond the Prison Walls: Preparing for Reentry

For many incarcerated individuals, release from prison is both a hopeful and daunting transition [116–118]. The outside world, despite its promise of freedom, presents its own set of challenges. Many individuals face barriers to employment, housing, and social reintegration. Without adequate support, the risk of recidivism is high. However, for those who have engaged in trauma-informed yoga, the practice becomes a tool they can carry with them beyond the prison walls.

The skills developed through yoga—self-regulation, patience, and mindfulness—are invaluable during the reentry process. The ability to pause and take a breath before responding to a stressful situation can mean the difference between escalating a conflict and finding a constructive resolution. The capacity to recognize and manage emotions can make it easier to navigate relationships and rebuild trust with family members. And the sense of self-worth cultivated through yoga can serve as a counterbalance to the external challenges of reentry.

Participants described ways that mindfulness helped with emotional regulation and impulse control. Andre stated:

> I thought it was about the poses and stuff, but it turned out that yoga wasn't about poses. Yoga was more about the self-regulation part. When you are in the pose, you want to give up and quit, but yoga taught me to breathe through that. Now that I'm out here, and (there are times that) I feel so mad, I'm so angry. I want to say a lot of stuff. I want to tell a lot of people a lot of stuff. But I have to practice that self-regulation..

In some cases, formerly incarcerated individuals have gone on to become yoga teachers themselves, using their experience to give back to others who are still navigating the system. These individuals serve as powerful examples of how healing and transformation are possible, even in the face of systemic oppression.

3.3.4 The Transformational Power of Ethical Relationship

At its core, the healing nature of an ethical relationship in trauma-informed yoga is about recognition—the recognition of humanity in a space that seeks to erase it. The facilitator, by showing up with presence, respect, and consistency, becomes a beacon of what is possible: connection, safety, and self-discovery.

In a system designed to punish rather than rehabilitate, trauma-informed yoga is an act of quiet revolution. It challenges the idea that incarcerated individuals are beyond redemption. It provides tools for healing that extend far beyond the yoga mat. And most importantly, it creates relationships that affirm one simple but radical truth: every person, regardless of their past, is worthy of healing.

This is the essence of an ethical relationship—not just in yoga, but in the broader fight for justice and human dignity. If we are to create a world in which healing is possible for all, we must first recognize the inherent worth of every individual, especially those whom society has cast aside. Through the simple, profound act of holding space, we begin to create that world, one breath, one movement, one ethical relationship at a time.

Chapter 4
Blending Disciplines: Integrating Research, Theory, and Practice in Trauma-Informed Yoga

Healing from trauma is not a linear process. It requires a multifaceted approach that acknowledges the complexity of the human experience—our neurological wiring, our emotional landscapes, and our lived histories. In this sense, trauma-informed yoga is not merely a standalone practice; it is the convergence of multiple disciplines, each contributing a critical piece to the puzzle of healing. From developmental psychology to neuroscience, from mindfulness research to embodiment practices, the integration of these fields has created a more comprehensive understanding of how trauma is stored in the body and how it can be released. Trauma-informed yoga, at its best, draws from this interdisciplinary foundation, blending ancient wisdom with modern science to create an approach that is both deeply personal and profoundly transformative. This chapter explores the wealth of research that informs trauma-informed embodiment practices, illustrating how the blending of disciplines leads to more effective interventions for those healing from trauma, particularly within incarcerated and marginalized communities.

4.1 Understanding Trauma in Incarcerated Populations: A Developmental and Neuroscientific Perspective

Incarcerated populations often have disproportionately high Adverse Childhood Experiences (ACE) scores, reflecting histories of trauma that have shaped their physiological and psychological responses to stress. The prison system itself perpetuates this state of hypervigilance, reinforcing patterns of fear, reactivity, and dissociation. Trauma-informed yoga directly addresses these issues by offering practices that engage both the body and mind in regulating the nervous system.

Neuroscience supports the idea that mindful movement, breathwork, and meditation can rewire neural pathways. Studies in neuroplasticity show that repeated engagement in mindfulness practices strengthens the connections between the

C. Williams, *Yoga in Prisons*, SpringerBriefs in Offending Populations & Correctional Psychotherapy, https://doi.org/10.1007/978-3-031-98368-9_4

prefrontal cortex and the limbic system, improving emotion regulation and reducing impulsivity [119]. This research provides a scientific basis for why trauma-informed yoga can be effective—it is not just about relaxation, but about retraining the brain to respond to stress in healthier ways.

4.2 Mindfulness as a Bridge to Healing

Mindfulness, defined as the practice of paying attention to the present moment without judgment, has been widely studied for its impact on mental health and trauma recovery. Mindfulness-based programs such as Mindfulness-Based Stress Reduction (MBSR) and Mindfulness-Based Cognitive Therapy (MBCT) have demonstrated effectiveness in reducing symptoms of PTSD, anxiety, and depression [120–124]. Trauma-informed yoga integrates mindfulness not only as a mental practice but as an embodied experience. Instead of simply observing thoughts, participants are invited to observe sensations in the body, to notice where tension resides, and to approach these sensations with curiosity rather than fear. This approach is critical for individuals with trauma, as it helps them rebuild a relationship with their own bodies—one that is often severed due to past harm.

Several studies have validated the effects of mindfulness-based interventions in prison populations. One study found that incarcerated individuals who participated in a mindfulness program showed significant improvements in emotional regulation, impulse control, and overall psychological well-being [125]. These findings align with broader research suggesting that mindfulness reduces activity in the amygdala—the brain's fear center—while increasing activation in the prefrontal cortex, leading to better decision-making and stress management [126].

Mindfulness also plays a key role in reducing recidivism. When individuals develop the ability to pause and observe their reactions rather than acting on impulse, they are less likely to engage in behaviors that lead to re-incarceration. Trauma-informed yoga, by integrating mindfulness with movement, provides a structured way for individuals to practice self-awareness and emotional regulation in real-time. Jack offered this explanation as to how the practice supports him during challenges times: "The breathing techniques and the sound of the facilitator's voice in my head (telling me over and over, I wish I could grant you a peaceful and painless life, but since I can't… I give you yoga) are two of the most powerful tools for success in the 6 months I have been out in society." Jake's journey illustrates the profound potential of yoga to facilitate inner transformation, even within the harshest of environments. His newfound ability to cultivate equanimity and compassion underscores how mindfulness practices can disrupt cycles of reactivity and violence, offering instead pathways toward healing and connection. Yet, Jake's story is not unique. His experiences echo those of many others who have engaged with yoga programs in carceral settings, discovering tools for self-regulation, emotional resilience, and personal growth. To deepen this understanding, the following chapters will present the voices of additional participants, along with findings from a qualitative study that examines the broader impact of yoga within prison contexts. Through these stories and insights, the potential of yoga to support healing and rehabilitation will come into sharper focus.

4.3 Embodiment Practices: Reclaiming the Body as a Safe Space

One of the most powerful aspects of trauma-informed yoga is its emphasis on embodiment—the process of fully inhabiting one's body with awareness and intention. Trauma often causes individuals to dissociate from their bodies as a means of self-protection. For those who have experienced physical or sexual abuse, or who have endured the chronic stress of incarceration, the body may feel like a place of pain rather than safety. Embodiment practices help reverse this disconnect by encouraging individuals to engage with their bodies in a way that feels empowering rather than overwhelming. Somatic experiencing, a therapeutic approach, is one such practice that informs trauma-informed yoga [127]. Research into Somatic Experiencing (SE) suggests that trauma is not just a psychological wound but a physiological one—unresolved energy becomes trapped in the body, leading to chronic tension, pain, and dysregulation. Through mindful movement, breathwork, and grounding techniques, trauma-informed yoga helps release this trapped energy in a safe and gradual way.

Research on the effects of yoga-based embodiment practices shows promising results. A study found that yoga was more effective than traditional talk therapy in reducing symptoms of PTSD, particularly in individuals who had experienced complex trauma [128]. The reason for this is simple: while talk therapy relies on verbal processing, yoga engages the body directly, bypassing the need for cognitive articulation and instead allowing for healing through movement and breath. In prison settings, where individuals are subjected to regimented schedules, bodily control, and intrusive surveillance, the act of moving freely—even within the limitations of a small space—can be a radical act of self-liberation. Simple poses, such as standing with feet firmly planted on the ground or taking deep diaphragmatic breaths, can create a profound shift in how an individual relates to their own body.

4.4 Blending the Wisdom of Science and Tradition

The integration of neuroscience, mindfulness, and embodiment practices within trauma-informed yoga reflects a larger movement in the field of mental health and rehabilitation—one that acknowledges the necessity of blending modern science with ancient wisdom. Yoga, which has been practiced for thousands of years as a tool for self-regulation and spiritual awakening, is now being validated by empirical research as a powerful intervention for trauma recovery. However, the blending of disciplines does not mean diluting the essence of yoga into a purely clinical intervention. Instead, it calls for a holistic approach—one that respects the depth of yoga's philosophical teachings while also embracing scientific advancements in understanding trauma and healing. The yamas and niyamas, the ethical foundations of yoga, align seamlessly with modern principles of trauma recovery, emphasizing self-compassion, nonviolence, and personal integrity [121, 129]. This interdisciplinary approach allows for greater accessibility and impact, particularly for marginalized populations. By recognizing that healing is both an art and a science, trauma-informed yoga becomes a bridge—connecting individuals to their bodies, to their breath, and to a larger framework of understanding that acknowledges their wholeness, rather than defining them by their past trauma.

4.5 Expanding the Integration: Moving Beyond Traditional Boundaries

The blending of disciplines in trauma-informed yoga is not just about incorporating neuroscience, mindfulness, and embodiment practices—it is about expanding the reach of healing modalities beyond traditional settings and making them accessible to those who need them most. Historically, trauma recovery has been confined to talk therapy, pharmacological interventions, or behavioral modification programs. While these approaches have their place, they often fall short for individuals whose trauma is deeply embodied. By integrating the insights of somatic psychology, developmental theory, and social justice frameworks, trauma-informed yoga practitioners and facilitators can offer a more comprehensive and inclusive approach. This is especially important for marginalized communities, including incarcerated individuals, who often lack access to quality mental health care but are disproportionately affected by trauma.

Prison systems, by design, do not prioritize healing, they reinforce cycles of harm, perpetuate racial and economic disparities, and limit access to rehabilitative services [8, 112]. In many ways, trauma-informed yoga challenges these structures by offering an alternative—a space where self-awareness, autonomy, and healing are prioritized over punishment. But for this work to have a lasting impact, it must move beyond isolated yoga sessions and become part of a broader movement that includes public health initiatives, policy reform, and community-based interventions.

4.6 The Role of Community and Social Connection in Healing

One of the most overlooked aspects of trauma recovery is the role of social connection. Research in developmental psychology and attachment theory suggests that relationships are critical to healing from trauma. Human beings are wired for connection; yet, many trauma survivors, especially those who are incarcerated, have experienced profound relational ruptures. Trauma-informed yoga, when practiced within a group setting, has the potential to rebuild these connections. The simple act of moving and breathing together fosters a sense of belonging—a critical element for individuals who have been isolated, whether through incarceration, addiction, or other life circumstances. Studies on group-based interventions, such as Yoga for Recovery (YFR), Yoga of 12-Step Recovery (Y12SR), and Mindfulness-Based Relapse Prevention (MBRP), show that the communal aspect of practice enhances resilience and reduces feelings of loneliness and shame [140].

In prison settings, where social interactions are often fraught with tension and hypervigilance, yoga offers a rare moment of collective healing. Participants learn to attune to their own bodies while also developing a sense of shared humanity with those around them. This shift from isolation to connection is critical for long-term healing, as it allows individuals to experience trust, cooperation, and emotional safety—perhaps for the first time in their lives. Beyond the prison walls, trauma-informed yoga programs can serve as a bridge to reintegration. Many individuals struggle with reentry, facing stigma, economic hardship, and a lack of support systems. Community-based yoga initiatives, particularly those led by formerly incarcerated individuals, provide continuity of care and a sense of belonging post-release. Programs such as the yoga classes have demonstrated that when incarcerated individuals receive training to become yoga teachers themselves, they not only deepen their own healing but also become leaders in the rehabilitation of others.

4.7 Embodiment as a Form of Social Justice

Trauma does not exist in a vacuum. It is shaped by social conditions, historical oppression, and systemic inequities. The high rates of trauma among incarcerated populations are not coincidental—they are the result of policies and structures that disproportionately criminalize poverty, mental illness, and racialized communities. Recognizing this, trauma-informed yoga must also be understood as a form of social justice. Embodiment is inherently political. To reclaim one's body in a system that has sought to control it is an act of resistance. Practices that encourage autonomy, choice, and self-regulation challenge the very foundations of incarceration, which rely on disempowerment and compliance. By fostering a sense of agency in participants, trauma-informed yoga disrupts the narrative that incarcerated individuals are beyond redemption. It affirms their capacity for healing, self-awareness, and transformation.

In this way, trauma-informed yoga practitioners are not just facilitators of healing, they are advocates for a more humane, rehabilitative approach to justice. They recognize that addressing trauma requires systemic change, not just individual interventions. This perspective aligns with emerging fields such as restorative justice and community-based trauma healing, which emphasize healing over punishment, relationships over isolation, and dignity over degradation. By blending disciplines, drawing from neuroscience, psychology, social justice, and somatic therapies, trauma-informed yoga offers a framework that is both deeply personal and profoundly societal. It acknowledges that trauma is not just an individual experience but a collective issue that requires collective healing.

4.8 The Future of Trauma-Informed Yoga: Expanding Access and Research

As trauma-informed yoga continues to gain recognition, there is a growing need for expanded access and further research. While existing studies highlight the benefits of yoga for trauma recovery, much of this research has been conducted in controlled settings, often with middle-class populations. More studies are needed to examine the long-term effects of trauma-informed yoga in diverse, real-world environments, including prisons, juvenile detention centers, shelters, and marginalized communities.

Policy change is also essential. While some correctional facilities have begun integrating mindfulness and yoga programs, many remain resistant, viewing these practices as luxuries rather than necessities. Advocates must work to shift this perception by demonstrating that trauma-informed yoga is not just about relaxation—it is about rehabilitation, emotional regulation, and breaking cycles of harm.

Additionally, training for facilitators must continue to evolve. Teaching yoga in trauma-sensitive environments requires a skill set that goes beyond traditional teacher training. Facilitators must be educated in trauma theory, cultural and structural competency, and ethical relationship-building. They must also be prepared to navigate institutional challenges, including resistance from prison staff and the logistical barriers of working in carceral settings.

Finally, the movement for trauma-informed yoga must include voices from within the communities it serves. Formerly incarcerated individuals who have experienced the transformative power of yoga should be empowered to take leadership roles. Their lived experience offers invaluable insight into how these programs can be most effectively implemented and sustained.

4.9 Blending Disciplines to Foster a New Paradigm of Healing

The integration of developmental research, mindfulness-based practices, and somatic and embodiment theories within trauma-informed yoga is not just an academic exercise—it is a necessary evolution of healing practices. By blending disciplines, we create a more holistic, effective, and inclusive approach to trauma recovery—one that acknowledges the complexities of the human nervous system, the impact of social conditions, and the profound potential for self-transformation. For incarcerated individuals, who have been systematically stripped of autonomy, dignity, and connection, trauma-informed yoga offers something revolutionary: the chance to reclaim their bodies, their breath, and their sense of self-worth. It provides a pathway to healing that is not dependent on external validation or approval but is instead rooted in their own inner experience.

By continuing to expand this work—through research, policy advocacy, community engagement, and facilitator training—we move closer to a world in which healing is not a privilege but a right. A world in which trauma is met not with punishment, but with compassion. A world in which the blending of disciplines leads to the blending of lives—where those who have been cast aside by society are given the opportunity to heal, to grow, and to redefine their futures. In the end, trauma-informed yoga is more than just a practice. It is a movement—one that challenges us to rethink what healing looks like, who it belongs to, and how we can collectively create environments that support transformation. The blending of disciplines is not just a methodology; it is a philosophy—one that recognizes that true healing is never singular, but always interconnected.

4.10 Beyond the Mat: The Evolution of Trauma-Informed Healing

The blending of disciplines in trauma-informed yoga is not just about integrating science, mindfulness, and embodiment—it is about reimagining healing itself. Trauma, particularly for incarcerated individuals, is not simply a psychological or physiological experience; it is a systemic wound, shaped by racial, economic, and social disparities. To effectively address trauma, we must expand our understanding beyond the individual level and consider how structural oppression, community disconnection, and generational cycles of harm contribute to its persistence. The movement for trauma-informed healing requires a shift in perspective—from seeing trauma as something that resides solely within an individual to recognizing it as a reflection of larger societal imbalances. This chapter explores the ways in which blending disciplines is not only reshaping the conversation around trauma but also inspiring new paradigms of justice, rehabilitation, and community restoration.

4.11 Trauma-Informed Yoga as a Pathway to Restorative Justice

Restorative justice is an approach to criminal justice that emphasizes healing over punishment, reconciliation over retribution, and community accountability over state-enforced discipline. Unlike traditional punitive systems, which focus on isolating and punishing individuals who commit crimes, restorative justice seeks to repair the harm done to individuals and communities through dialogue, accountability, and collective healing.

The principles of restorative justice align closely with those of trauma-informed yoga. Both recognize the profound impact of trauma on human behavior, acknowledging that many individuals who end up in the criminal justice system are not inherently "bad" but are instead responding to a lifetime of unhealed wounds. Trauma-informed yoga works within this framework by helping individuals reconnect with their bodies, regulate their emotions, and cultivate a sense of personal agency—critical skills for those who are engaged in restorative justice processes.

Programs that integrate yoga into restorative justice initiatives have shown promising results. For example, some correctional facilities have implemented yoga and mindfulness practices alongside victim-offender dialogue programs, allowing participants to engage in deep self-reflection before entering facilitated discussions about their past actions. This combination of movement, breathwork, and restorative dialogue has been found to improve participants' ability to process guilt, navigate difficult emotions, and approach reconciliation with greater emotional resilience. By blending trauma-informed yoga with restorative justice, we move closer to a justice system that acknowledges harm while still prioritizing healing. Rather than reinforcing cycles of punishment and trauma, this approach offers a way forward—one that is rooted in both accountability and the possibility of transformation.

4.12 Cultural Sensitivity and the Decolonization of Healing Practices

As trauma-informed yoga expands into marginalized and incarcerated communities, it is essential to recognize the need for cultural sensitivity and the decolonization of healing practices. Yoga, though widely practiced in the West, has roots in South Asian spiritual traditions that have often been appropriated, diluted, or commercialized for privileged audiences. Additionally, many modern trauma-informed therapeutic approaches are rooted in Western psychology, which may not fully account for the diverse ways that different cultures experience and heal from trauma.

To truly blend disciplines in a way that honors all individuals, trauma-informed yoga must be adapted to the specific cultural and historical contexts of those it seeks to serve. This means:

- **Honoring Indigenous and Ancestral Healing Practices**—Many cultures have long histories of somatic and community-based healing practices, from African drumming and dance to Native American sweat lodges and prayer rituals. Trauma-informed yoga should seek to complement, rather than replace, these traditions.
- **Addressing Racial Trauma and Historical Oppression**—Incarcerated individuals, particularly Black, Indigenous, and People of Color (BIPOC), often carry the compounded trauma of systemic racism, intergenerational poverty, and historical violence. Yoga programs must acknowledge these realities and create spaces where racialized trauma can be processed and healed.
- **Creating Inclusive and Accessible Practices**—Trauma-informed yoga should be available to all individuals, regardless of physical ability, gender identity, or socioeconomic status. This means offering variations for different bodies, using language that is free from bias, and ensuring that facilitators are representative of the communities they serve.

The future of trauma-informed healing requires a decolonized approach—one that respects the diverse ways in which different communities heal and integrates these perspectives into the practice itself.

4.13 The Role of Trauma-Informed Yoga in Reentry and Reintegration

For many incarcerated individuals, the journey does not end upon release—it only changes. Reentering society after incarceration presents a new set of challenges, from finding employment and housing to rebuilding relationships with family members and avoiding recidivism. Without adequate support, many individuals struggle to reintegrate, and the risk of returning to the prison system remains high.

Trauma-informed yoga can serve as a critical tool for reentry by offering formerly incarcerated individuals a means of self-regulation, empowerment, and community connection. Some of the most promising reentry programs are those that train individuals in yoga facilitation while they are still incarcerated, providing them with the skills to become teachers upon release. In addition to employment opportunities, yoga provides a much-needed emotional support system for individuals navigating reentry. The ability to manage stress through breathwork, move through anxiety with gentle postures, and find a sense of belonging in community-based yoga programs can make all the difference in reducing recidivism. Some reentry initiatives have even begun incorporating yoga into parole programs, allowing individuals to continue their practice as they transition back into society. The blending of trauma-informed yoga with reentry strategies represents a shift toward a more holistic approach to rehabilitation, one that sees individuals not as offenders but as people with the potential for healing and reintegration.

4.14 Expanding the Research: The Next Frontier of Trauma-Informed Yoga

While existing research highlights the benefits of trauma-informed yoga, there is still much work to be done. Many studies have focused on short-term outcomes, such as stress reduction and emotional regulation, but more longitudinal research is needed to explore the long-term impact of yoga on individuals who have experienced trauma.

Key areas for future research include:

- **The Impact on Recidivism Rates**—Can regular participation in trauma-informed yoga reduce the likelihood of reoffending?
- **Neurological Changes Over Time**—How does sustained yoga practice affect brain function in trauma survivors?
- **Intergenerational Healing**—Can yoga help break cycles of trauma that are passed down through families?
- **The Role of Peer-Led Programs**—How effective are trauma-informed yoga programs when they are taught by formerly incarcerated individuals to their peers?

By expanding the scope of research, we can continue refining trauma-informed yoga to better serve those who need it most.

4.15 A New Paradigm of Healing

The blending of disciplines in trauma-informed yoga is more than just an academic exercise—it is a radical reimagining of what healing can look like, who it belongs to, and how it can be integrated into systems that have historically perpetuated harm.

By drawing from neuroscience, developmental research, embodiment practices, restorative justice, and cultural healing traditions, we are creating a more expansive, inclusive, and effective approach to trauma recovery. This work is not just about reducing stress or improving flexibility—it is about restoring agency, dignity, and humanity to those who have been systematically devalued.

The future of trauma-informed yoga is one in which healing is not a privilege, but a right. A future in which every person—regardless of their past, their sentence, or their circumstances—has access to tools that help them reconnect with their body, their breath, and their sense of self.

Through the blending of disciplines, we are not just transforming individual lives—we are reshaping entire systems. We are proving that healing is possible, even in the most unlikely places. And, most importantly, we are affirming that every person, no matter their history, is worthy of that healing.

This is the promise of trauma-informed yoga. This is the power of blending disciplines. This is the future of embodied justice.

4.16 The Future of Trauma-Informed Embodiment Practices

As research continues to expand, the integration of mindfulness-based, trauma-informed embodiment practices will play an increasingly vital role in trauma recovery, particularly in prisons, rehabilitation centers, and marginalized communities. The evidence is clear: trauma is stored in the body, and healing must involve the body.

Blending disciplines allows for a more nuanced and effective approach to healing—one that acknowledges the complexity of trauma while offering accessible, evidence-based tools for resilience and self-regulation. Trauma-informed yoga is not just about movement; it is about rewriting the body's story, reclaiming autonomy, and fostering a sense of connection that transcends the limitations of the past. Through this integration, individuals are given the opportunity to not just survive, but to thrive.

Chapter 5
Breathing Truth, Being Alive

Breath is the most fundamental aspect of life. It is the first thing we do when we enter the world and the last thing we do before we leave it. Yet, for many who have endured trauma—especially those who are incarcerated—breath becomes something constricted, shallow, and disconnected from awareness. The body tightens, the chest tightens, and the nervous system remains trapped in a cycle of hypervigilance or shutdown. In this state, breathing is not a source of vitality; it is a survival mechanism, a minimal function that keeps the body alive but does little to support true healing.

In the practice of yoga, breath is not just a physiological function—it is a gateway to transformation [93]. Ancient yogic traditions have long recognized the breath as a bridge between the body and mind, between the conscious and the unconscious, between fear and freedom. Pranayama, the practice of breath control, offers a profound and accessible tool for addressing trauma. For incarcerated individuals, whose agency and autonomy have been stripped away, reclaiming the breath is an act of power. It is a return to presence, a quiet revolution that no external force can take away. In the harsh environment of prisons—where every movement is monitored, every action dictated, and the weight of confinement presses heavily on the spirit—breathing deeply, fully, and with awareness is an act of resistance. It is a way of saying: *I am here. I exist. I am alive.*

5.1 The Impact of Trauma on the Breath

Trauma fundamentally alters the way a person breathes [111, 121, 128]. For those who have experienced violence, neglect, abuse, or systemic oppression, the body learns to exist in a state of perpetual defense. The breath becomes shallow, centered in the upper chest rather than the deep belly. This is not a coincidence; it is a survival response. When danger is perceived—whether real or remembered—the nervous

C. Williams, *Yoga in Prisons*, SpringerBriefs in Offending Populations & Correctional Psychotherapy, https://doi.org/10.1007/978-3-031-98368-9_5

system triggers the *fight, flight, or freeze* response. The heart rate increases, the muscles tense, and the breath becomes rapid and constricted to prepare the body for action or protection.

For those who have been incarcerated, this state of hypervigilance becomes chronic. The prison environment itself is a constant trigger—loud noises, unpredictable interactions, threats of violence, and the complete lack of personal safety all reinforce the body's defensive patterns. Many incarcerated individuals experience dissociation, a numbing response to overwhelming trauma, which further disconnects them from their breath. Instead of breathing fully and consciously, they breathe just enough to get through the day. This is why breathwork—specifically, trauma-informed Pranayama—can be a powerful intervention. It works at the root level of the nervous system, offering a way to reset the physiological patterns of trauma. Unlike talk therapy, which requires verbal articulation of past experiences, breathwork bypasses the cognitive mind and works directly with the body's innate intelligence. It is a healing practice that requires no words, only presence.

5.2 Pranayama: The Science and Spirit of Breathwork

Pranayama, the yogic science of breath control, is one of the oldest and most revered practices in yoga [130]. The word itself comes from two Sanskrit roots: *Prana*, meaning life force or vital energy, and *Ayama*, meaning extension or expansion. Together, Pranayama refers to the conscious regulation of breath to expand and direct life energy. From a physiological standpoint, Pranayama directly influences the autonomic nervous system, shifting the body out of chronic stress and into a state of equilibrium. Different breath techniques activate different responses: some calm the nervous system, others energize it, and some create balance between the two. For incarcerated individuals, who exist in an environment that fosters chronic stress, learning to regulate their nervous system through breath is a profound act of self-empowerment.

But beyond the science, Pranayama is also a practice of truth. It reveals what is happening inside—the tension, the fear, the emotions that have been buried beneath years of survival. It offers an opportunity to face what has been avoided, to breathe into the places that have been constricted, and to slowly, gently, reclaim the body's natural rhythm.

5.3 Trauma-Informed Breath Practices for Incarcerated Populations

Not all breathwork is appropriate for trauma survivors. Certain Pranayama techniques that involve breath retention or forceful exhalation can be triggering for those who have experienced suffocation, panic attacks, or violence. A trauma-informed approach to Pranayama in prison settings focuses on accessible, grounding, and non-coercive techniques that help individuals feel safe in their own breath [11–14]. The practices shared here can be helpful for anyone, but especially for those who have experienced trauma. They can be found throughout all yoga traditions and texts, practiced for centuries by ancient yogis seeking enlightenment and the general public in search of better health and enhanced wellbeing [93, 131–136].

5.3.1 Deep Belly Breathing (Diaphragmatic Breath)

This is the foundation of all trauma-informed breath practices. Deep belly breathing engages the diaphragm and encourages the breath to move fully into the lower lungs, signaling to the nervous system that it is safe to relax.

How it works:

- The participant places one hand on the belly and the other on the chest.
- As they inhale, they send the breath deep into the belly, expanding it outward like a balloon.
- As they exhale, they allow the belly to gently fall.

This practice counteracts the shallow, rapid breathing associated with trauma and begins to rewire the body's stress response. It can be done anytime, anywhere—no mat, no special setting, just the body and breath.

5.3.2 Nadi Shodhana (Alternate Nostril Breathing)

This breathwork technique balances the two hemispheres of the brain and promotes a sense of inner stability. It is particularly useful for those experiencing racing thoughts, anxiety, or emotional overwhelm.

How it works:

- The participant closes the right nostril with the thumb and inhales deeply through the left nostril.
- They then close the left nostril with the ring finger and exhale through the right nostril.

- This alternation continues, moving the breath gently from side to side.

In a prison setting, where emotional regulation is often a struggle, this technique can serve as an anchor, bringing individuals back to center in moments of distress.

5.3.3 *Ujjayi (Ocean Breath)*

Ujjayi breath is known for its grounding and focusing effects. It is often used in yoga to maintain steadiness, but for trauma survivors, it serves as a tool for reclaiming control over the breath.

How it works:

- The participant inhales deeply through the nose, slightly constricting the back of the throat to create a whispering sound.
- The exhale is slow and controlled, maintaining the same constriction.

This breath mimics the natural sound of waves, creating a soothing effect that can be deeply comforting for individuals in high-stress environments.

5.4 Breath as Freedom

In a prison system that strips individuals of control, Pranayama offers something radical: the ability to regulate one's own internal state. It is a form of autonomy that no guard, no system, no institution can take away. It is a silent, invisible act of reclaiming power. For many incarcerated individuals, the first deep breath in years feels like an awakening. The body, long tense and guarded, begins to soften. The mind, long clouded by stress and survival, begins to clear. In these moments, breath becomes more than just oxygen—it becomes a declaration of life. To breathe fully is to acknowledge one's own existence. It is to say, *I am here, I am alive, and I deserve to be present in my own body.* And in the context of trauma, oppression, and incarceration, there is no truth more powerful than that. An example of this change emerged from how Jack's formal practice allowed him to access psychological states of self-regulation, which he has brought into challenging times. He described an example of feeling stressed in an encounter with a roommate at his current transitional facility:

> "This guy is talking about food. And he's bringing up incidents triggering me about me not cooking this or I should have cooked that. And so all these things are triggering me, and I physically feel a (sensation) equivalent to that crunch pose (garudasana or eagle pose). Right? I am triggered to the max! I'm tense; I'm barely breathing. I feel it in my hands. Like I'm about to punch him. Well, yoga class was like that, that feeling of intensity, where it's okay, and you can ease back down, you can hold that intensity for as long as you want. You

can breathe it out, you can slow down, and you can relax. I don't know how else to describe it; like I said, it was profound."

Jack's experience powerfully illustrates how breath and breathwork can be profound tools for liberation, both in the body and in daily life. Amid a triggering confrontation with a roommate, he became acutely aware of how stress manifested physiologically: tight muscles, clenched fists, shallow breathing, and the urge toward violence. Rather than reacting impulsively, he drew upon his embodied memory of breath-centered yoga practice. Jack recognized the internal state, and recalled how, in class, he learned to stay with that intensity without collapsing into it or fleeing from it. The breath became his anchor and his guide: a means to regulate, to pause, and to re-enter the moment with choice rather than reaction. In this way, the breath served not only as a somatic tool, but as a pathway to self-mastery and liberation—freeing him from the unconscious cycles of reactivity and harm that incarceration so often reinforces. Jack's story reveals that through intentional breathwork, even in confined spaces, one can experience spaciousness, self-possession, and the profound possibility of transformation.

While breathing is an autonomic process, conscious breathing uniquely engages the brain and the breather. Findings suggest that breathing can act as a hierarchical organizing principle for neuronal oscillations throughout the brain and detail mechanisms of how cognitive factors impact otherwise automatic neuronal processes during interoceptive attention. Manuel offered:

To be sincere, it took me a few years to start seeing the difference, to feeling the benefits. For instance, my breathing became my best friend. Unconsciously, my breath became something I would lean on and connect with inside myself.

Manuel's reflection illustrates the deeply transformative potential of breath as both a physiological anchor and a spiritual ally on the path toward liberation. His words—"my breathing became my best friend"—signal a shift from breath as a mere biological function to breath as an intimate and reliable companion. This transformation aligns with emerging neuroscientific findings that suggest breathing is not only central to physiological regulation but also serves as a hierarchical organizing principle for brain activity, modulating neuronal oscillations that influence attention, emotion, and self-awareness. Over time, Manuel's unconscious return to his breath reflects the development of interoceptive awareness, where internal signals like respiration become tools for resilience and grounding. In a carceral environment marked by hypervigilance and disconnection, his ability to connect with his breath provided him with an internal refuge, a means to self-regulate amidst chaos, and a subtle yet powerful reclaiming of agency. As such, the breath becomes more than a practice, it becomes a portal to freedom within, even in the most externally constrained conditions.

The educational component of the yoga classes was often cited in the participant's responses, emphasizing the material's impact and integration. Manuel explained:

> [I] also realized how true the concept "The Body Keeps the Score" (a reference to the book by Dr. Bessel van der Kolk) was an experience. I could not have previously imagined. With time, my practice was something that I looked forward to every week.

He described how he used the practice during the week to "stay vigilant with my thoughts, speech, and actions." With practice, he found that the breath practice came naturally, explaining:

It helped tremendously in my everyday life. To this day, I can say that I would not be the mindful person that I am today if it was not for the Sangha (Sanskrit word meaning "spiritual community") that helped me become who I am today.

This reflection demonstrates how the breath becomes both a tool and a teacher, guiding the practitioner toward mindful awareness in daily life. His ability to "stay vigilant" with thoughts, speech, and actions illustrates the ethical clarity that emerges when breathwork becomes an embodied habit. Importantly, he credits the sangha—the spiritual community—as foundational to this transformation. In the isolating environment of incarceration, this sense of belonging and mutual support provided a structure through which inner discipline could take root. The practice, grounded in breath and nurtured in community, became a path toward self-liberation—a means of becoming, in his words, "the mindful person I am today." This evolution reflects the power of relational healing and contemplative practice to restore agency, dignity, and self-respect even under carceral conditions.

5.5 The Power of Breath: Reclaiming the Present Moment

For individuals who have lived through trauma, particularly those who are incarcerated, the ability to remain present is often compromised. The mind is frequently caught in cycles of fear, regret, or hypervigilance, anticipating the next threat or replaying past pain. This dissociation from the present moment is not just psychological—it is deeply physiological. The nervous system, conditioned by repeated stressors, remains in a state of either chronic activation (*fight-or-flight*) or collapse (*freeze*).

Breathing practices, particularly trauma-informed Pranayama, serve as an anchor to the present. Unlike traditional meditation, which can feel inaccessible or overwhelming for trauma survivors, focusing on the breath provides a tangible, immediate point of connection. There is no pressure to "clear the mind" or relive painful memories. Instead, breathwork invites the practitioner to notice:

- *What does this inhale feel like?*
- *Where is tension being held in the body?*
- *What happens when I exhale just a little longer than usual?*

These micro-moments of awareness help to reestablish a sense of presence without force. The breath does not demand. It does not judge. It simply exists as a constant companion, a reminder that the present moment is still available, no matter how much the past has dictated one's life.

For those who are incarcerated, where every day is structured by external forces—guards, rules, schedules—the ability to claim ownership of even a single breath is a radical act of self-empowerment. It is a reclaiming of time, space, and self.

5.6 A Breath-Based Path Forward

Breathwork, as part of trauma-informed yoga in prisons, is more than just a calming practice. It is a vehicle for transformation, a tool for survival, and a means of reclaiming the self. It is a way of practicing presence in a system designed to keep individuals disconnected.

By engaging with breathwork, incarcerated individuals develop:

- **Greater Emotional Regulation**—The ability to manage stress, anger, and fear through conscious breathing rather than reactive outbursts.
- **A Sense of Agency**—The recognition that they can influence their own nervous system, thoughts, and reactions, even within the constraints of incarceration.
- **Connection to the Present Moment**—The ability to find stillness, even in an environment of chaos and control.
- **A Pathway to Healing**—The opportunity to reprogram the body's response to trauma, creating new patterns of relaxation and self-awareness.

Pranayama does not promise immediate transformation. Healing from trauma, especially within the prison system, is not linear. But every breath taken with awareness is a step toward healing. Every conscious inhale is an act of self-care. Every extended exhale is a release of tension that has been held for too long.

And so, breath by breath, those who engage in these practices begin to cultivate a new way of being—one that is not dictated by the past, not defined by the prison system, but rooted in the simple, undeniable truth:

I am here. I am breathing. I am alive.

Chapter 6
Healing Justice: The Role of Integrative Health Equity in Providing Inclusive Care for Incarcerated Populations

Justice, in its truest sense, extends beyond punishment and accountability. True justice must also include healing—healing for individuals, healing for communities, and healing for the systemic wounds inflicted by inequality, racism, and generational trauma. In the context of incarceration, where human dignity is often sacrificed in the name of control, the concept of **healing justice** emerges as a revolutionary framework. It challenges the traditional punitive model and instead asks: *What if justice also meant restoration? What if accountability included healing? What if rehabilitation was centered on care rather than punishment?*

At the intersection of justice and healing lies **integrative health equity**—an approach that recognizes the deep disparities in health care access and outcomes for marginalized communities, including incarcerated individuals. Trauma-informed, mindfulness-based yoga is one of the most powerful tools within this framework. By integrating somatic healing, emotional regulation, and mindful awareness, this practice has the potential to address the profound physical, mental, and emotional wounds carried by those within the prison system.

Incarceration does not just remove people from society—it strips them of autonomy, bodily agency, and access to meaningful health care. If we are to truly seek justice, then we must also seek to heal those who have been most harmed by systemic oppression, poverty, racial injustice, and intergenerational trauma. **This is the work of healing justice.**

Healing justice demands a response to these injustices. It calls for an approach that does not just manage symptoms but seeks to address the root causes of suffering. This is where trauma-informed, mindfulness-based yoga becomes a critical tool for **integrative health equity**—bringing healing practices to those who have been denied them for too long. Leroy felt that his yoga practice helps him maintain his health. "Yoga helps me with hypertension. So, it (yoga) has many benefits for the physical body. Instead of taking pills, I do yoga." The stories recounted by the participants provided compelling evidence that yoga can be an effective tool for maintaining the health of incarcerated individuals and treating various ailments,

C. Williams, *Yoga in Prisons*, SpringerBriefs in Offending Populations & Correctional Psychotherapy, https://doi.org/10.1007/978-3-031-98368-9_6

empowering them to take an active role in managing their health and its physical benefits. Regularly practicing yoga gave them a sense of control and agency over their health. These accounts emphasized incorporating yoga into correctional facilities to improve incarcerated individuals' health outcomes and promote well-being.

6.1 Integrative Health Equity: A Model for Inclusive Healing

Integrative health equity is more than just an ideal; it is a necessary shift in how we approach health care for marginalized populations, particularly those who are incarcerated [137, 138]. Through the lens of integrative health equity, health and healthcare for incarcerated people becomes a model that:

- Recognizes **trauma as a root cause of illness**
- Centers **healing rather than punishment**
- Makes **wellness accessible** to all, regardless of race, gender, or socioeconomic background
- Integrates **mindfulness, movement, and community-based healing**

A **trauma-informed, mindfulness-based yoga program** in prisons aligns with these principles in powerful ways. Unlike traditional prison health care, which often focuses on controlling symptoms with medication, **yoga provides a pathway for self-healing, empowerment, and long-term transformation.**

6.1.1 A Call to Action: Reimagining Justice Through Healing

The current prison system is failing. It is failing individuals, it is failing communities, and it is failing society. But there is a path forward—one that prioritizes **integrative health equity, trauma-informed care, and healing justice.**

To move toward this vision, we must:

1. **Expand Trauma-Informed Yoga Programs in Prisons, Jails and Re-Entry Facilities**
    - Advocate for **state-funded wellness and rehabilitation initiatives** that incorporate yoga and mindfulness.
    - Train facilitators in **trauma-sensitive teaching** to ensure that yoga is accessible and inclusive.
    - Work with prison administrations to **integrate yoga into existing mental health and rehabilitation services.**
2. **Shift Policy to Support Healing-Centered Criminal Justice Reform**
    - Advocate for **mental health services over punitive measures** in legal sentencing.

- Push for **alternatives to incarceration**, such as restorative justice programs, that focus on **accountability and healing** rather than punishment.
- Ensure that formerly incarcerated individuals have **access to trauma-informed health care post-release**.

3. **Educate the Public on the Importance of Healing Justice**

- Challenge the **misconception that rehabilitation is a privilege** rather than a necessity.
- Raise awareness about **the link between trauma and incarceration**—and how **healing interventions can prevent crime at its root**.
- Build partnerships between **yoga organizations, criminal justice reform advocates, and public health professionals** to promote **integrative approaches** to justice.

6.1.2 A Future Built on Healing, Not Harm

Healing justice is **not a utopian dream; it is a necessity for a just society**. If we truly want safer communities, if we truly want rehabilitation, if we genuinely believe in human dignity, then we must **integrate healing into the very fabric of our justice system**.

Trauma-informed, mindfulness-based yoga is **one piece of a much larger movement**—a movement that seeks to **restore rather than punish, to heal rather than harm, and to build a world where justice means transformation, not suffering**.

The path forward is clear. The work is urgent.

Because **true justice is not just about what we take away, it is about what we rebuild, breath by breath, life by life.**

Chapter 7

The Path Ahead: Putting Healing Justice into Practice

> **"Everything beautiful about this life contains a secret, something invisible, sacred in the depths of its heart",**
> Donald Kalsched, Ph.D., Trauma and the Soul [139]

The concept of **healing justice** calls for a radical reimagining of how we approach incarceration, rehabilitation, and health equity. It challenges us to move beyond punitive models of justice and instead prioritize **trauma healing, emotional regulation, and holistic well-being** for incarcerated populations. The research is clear: trauma-informed, mindfulness-based yoga is an effective tool for self-regulation, nervous system healing, and emotional resilience. But knowledge alone is not enough. The next step—the path ahead—is about **application, advocacy, and systemic change**.

This chapter serves as a **guide for practitioners, clinicians, policymakers, and advocates** who want to integrate healing justice into their work. Whether you are a **yoga teacher, mental health professional, social worker, criminal justice advocate, or correctional facility administrator**, this chapter will offer tangible ways to **put this knowledge into practice** and become an active participant in the movement for healing-centered rehabilitation.

7.1 The Breath of Liberation: A Call for Healing Justice

At the heart of this book lies a fundamental truth: healing and justice are not opposing forces—they are inextricably linked. To heal is to create the conditions for true justice. To seek justice without healing is to perpetuate cycles of harm, trauma, and oppression.

Through the lens of trauma-informed, mindfulness-based yoga, we have explored the profound intersections between incarceration, trauma, and healing. We have examined the realities of prison life—environments that strip individuals of autonomy, dignity, and access to meaningful care. We have delved into the science and

C. Williams, *Yoga in Prisons*, SpringerBriefs in Offending Populations & Correctional Psychotherapy, https://doi.org/10.1007/978-3-031-98368-9_7

spirituality of breath, movement, and mindfulness as tools for reclaiming one's body, regulating emotions, and fostering resilience. And most importantly, we have reimagined a world in which rehabilitation is not an afterthought, but the very foundation of justice.

As we reach the conclusion of this journey, one question remains: Where do we go from here?

7.2 Reframing the Narrative: From Punishment to Possibility

For too long, society has been conditioned to see incarceration as the natural consequence of wrongdoing, as the unavoidable fate of those who "deserve" it. But incarceration is not just the result of individual actions—it is the outcome of systemic failures.

- The failure to address childhood trauma.
- The failure to provide equitable education, healthcare, and economic opportunities.
- The failure to offer alternatives to incarceration that focus on healing rather than punishment.

If the goal of the justice system were truly rehabilitation, then prisons would look nothing like they do today. They would not be places of violence, deprivation, and despair. They would be spaces of healing, accountability, and growth—designed to break, rather than reinforce, cycles of harm.

This book has laid out a vision for what that kind of justice could look like. A justice system that recognizes trauma as both a cause and consequence of incarceration. A justice system that invests in the well-being of individuals rather than their suffering. A justice system that understands true accountability is not about isolation—it is about transformation.

Trauma-informed, mindfulness-based yoga is one powerful tool in this broader vision of healing justice. It offers an embodied pathway to reclaiming self-worth, restoring autonomy, and reprogramming the nervous system after years—often decades—of survival mode. It is not a luxury or an indulgence. It is a necessity for any system that seeks to truly rehabilitate.

7.3 Healing Is Liberation: The Radical Power of Breath and Movement

To breathe deeply is to affirm one's existence. To move freely is to reclaim one's body from the grip of trauma. These are acts of resistance in a system designed to control, suppress, and disconnect individuals from their own humanity.

Throughout this book, we have seen how trauma-informed yoga fosters emotional regulation, self-awareness, and resilience among incarcerated individuals. We have seen how simple breathing practices can offer relief from PTSD, anxiety, and chronic stress. We have seen how mindfulness cultivates presence, allowing individuals to respond rather than react, to observe rather than be consumed by their pain.

The true power of these practices is that they belong to the individual. They cannot be taken away, confined, or controlled. No prison system, no sentence, no external authority can strip a person of their breath. It is theirs alone—a personal revolution, a quiet liberation.

For those who have spent their lives feeling powerless, the realization that they can control their own internal state—even in an environment where everything else is dictated—is profound. It is a reminder that they are more than their worst decisions, more than their past traumas, more than a system that has sought to reduce them to a number. Healing justice begins with this reclaiming of self. And from this place of self-connection, a ripple effect begins.

7.4 From the Individual to the Collective: A Ripple Effect of Healing

While this book has largely focused on the individual experience of yoga in prisons, the impact of healing justice extends far beyond the self.

When an individual learns to self-regulate, to process emotions, to replace anger with awareness, they transform their interactions with others.

- Fewer conflicts within prison walls.
- Healthier relationships with family and community members' post-release.
- A shift in prison culture—from one of survival to one of shared healing.

When enough individuals experience this transformation, the system itself begins to change. Prison yoga programs are already challenging the status quo, proving that rehabilitation is possible when people are given the right tools. Some formerly incarcerated individuals have even gone on to become yoga teachers themselves, bringing the practice back to their communities, ensuring that healing does not stop at the prison gate.

This is how systemic change begins—not through punishment and fear, but through compassion and empowerment.

7.5 Conclusion

A Call to Action: The Future of Healing Justice

This book is not just an exploration, it is a call to action. The path toward healing justice requires all of us.

- If you are a yoga teacher, consider bringing trauma-informed yoga into carceral and rehabilitative settings.
- If you are an advocate for criminal justice reform, push for policies that integrate holistic rehabilitation into prison programming.
- If you are an educator, incorporate trauma-informed mindfulness into your teaching to support at-risk youth before they enter the prison system.
- If you are a mental health professional, support embodied healing practices for populations that have been historically denied care.
- If you are someone who simply believes in the power of transformation, share this knowledge—challenge the narrative that prisons must be places of suffering rather than spaces for rehabilitation.

Healing justice is not just about prisons. It is about breaking the cycles of harm that lead to incarceration in the first place. It is about recognizing that trauma, when unaddressed, continues to cause harm—both to the individual and to society at large.

We must ask ourselves: What kind of world do we want to create?

A world where harm is met with more harm? Or a world where harm is met with the possibility of repair?

A world where people are discarded? Or a world where people are given the tools to heal, grow, and contribute?

Healing justice is not an idealistic dream—it is a necessity for a just society. It is the only path forward if we truly believe in rehabilitation, public safety, and human dignity.

7.6 Final Breath: Justice, Presence, and the Power of Now

If there is one lesson to take from this book, it is this:
Healing is always possible.
No matter how broken a system may seem.
No matter how lost a person may feel.
No matter how much harm has been inflicted.
The breath is always there, waiting to guide us back.
This is the lesson that incarcerated individuals learn when they step onto a yoga mat, when they take their first full breath in years, when they experience a moment of peace within a system of punishment.
It is the lesson we must all learn.
Justice without healing is incomplete. Healing without justice is unsustainable.
The two must walk hand in hand.
And when they do, we do not just change the lives of those inside prison walls.
We change the world itself.

References

1. Davis AY. Freedom is a constant struggle: Ferguson, Palestine, and the foundations of a movement. Haymarket Books; 2016.
2. McCartney PSD. Authenticity, legitimacy and the Transglobal yoga industry: a sociological analysis of Shanti Mandir. Taylor & Francis; 2025.
3. Bhalla N, O'Boyle J, Moscowitz L. Selling yoga 'off the mat': a 10-year analysis of lifestyle advertorials in yoga journal magazine. J Commun Inq. 2024;48(2):243–66. https://doi.org/10.1177/01968599221118646.
4. Finch AK. Black feminism and the practice of care. Palimpsest. 2022;11(1):1–41. 208
5. Fish A. The commodification and exchange of knowledge in the case of transnational commercial yoga. Int J Cult Prop. 2006;13(2):189–206.
6. Montross C. Waiting for an Echo: the madness of American incarceration. Penguin; 2020.
7. Raphael S, Stoll MA. Why are so many Americans in prison? Russell Sage Foundation; 2013.
8. Bauer S. American prison: a reporter's undercover journey into the business of punishment. Penguin; 2018.
9. Edelman P. Not a crime to be poor: the criminalization of poverty in America. The New Press; 2019.
10. Sawyer W, Wagner P. Mass incarceration: The Whole Pie 2025. 2025. https://www.prisonpolicy.org/reports/pie2025.html. Accessed 28 July 2025.
11. Auty KM, Cope A, Liebling A. A systematic review and meta-analysis of yoga and mindfulness meditation in prison. Int J Offender Ther Comp Criminol. 2017;61(6):689–710. https://doi.org/10.1177/0306624X15602514.
12. Bartels L, Oxman LN, Hopkins A. "I would just feel really relaxed and at peace": findings from a pilot prison yoga program in Australia. Int J Offender Ther Comp Criminol. 2019;63(15–16):2531–49. https://doi.org/10.1177/0306624X19854869.
13. Bilderbeck AC, Brazil IA, Farias M. Preliminary evidence that yoga practice progressively improves mood and decreases stress in a sample of UK prisoners. Evid Based Complement Alternat Med. 2015;2015:e819183. https://doi.org/10.1155/2015/819183.
14. Buric I, Farias M, Kurtev S, et al. Feasibility and preliminary outcomes of intensive mindfulness and yoga on prisoners with personality disorders: a randomised controlled preliminary study. Brain Behavior Immun Integr. 2023;2:100009. https://doi.org/10.1016/j.bbii.2023.100009.
15. Griera M. Yoga in penitentiary settings: transcendence, spirituality, and self-improvement. Hum Stud. 2017;40(1):77–100. https://doi.org/10.1007/s10746-016-9404-6.
16. Alexander M. The new Jim crow: mass incarceration in the age of colorblindness. The New Press; 2020.

C. Williams, *Yoga in Prisons*, SpringerBriefs in Offending Populations & Correctional Psychotherapy, https://doi.org/10.1007/978-3-031-98368-9

17. Monk EP. The color of punishment: African Americans, skin tone, and the criminal justice system. Ethn Racial Stud. 2019;42(10):1593–612. https://doi.org/10.1080/01419870.2018.1508736.
18. Nellis A. The color of justice: Racial and ethinic disparity in state prisons. Published online. 2021. https://www.sentencingproject.org/app/uploads/2022/08/The-Color-of-Justice-Racial-and-Ethnic-Disparity-in-State-Prisons.pdf
19. Wolff N, Caravaca SF. Associations among psychological distress, adverse childhood experiences, social support, and resilience in incarcerate men. Crim Justice Behav. 2019;46(11):1630–49. https://doi.org/10.1177/0093854819876008.
20. Wolff N, Shi J. Childhood and adult trauma experiences of incarcerated persons and their relationship to adult behavioral health problems and treatment. Int J Environ Res Public Health. 2012;9(5):1908–26. https://doi.org/10.3390/ijerph9051908.
21. Wolff N, Huening J, Shi J, Frueh BC. Trauma exposure and posttraumatic stress disorder among incarcerated M en. J Urban Health. 2014;91(4):707–19. https://doi.org/10.1007/s11524-014-9871-x.
22. Altintas M, Bilici M. Evaluation of childhood trauma with respect to criminal behavior, dissociative experiences, adverse family experiences and psychiatric backgrounds among prison inmates. Compr Psychiatry. 2018;82:100–7. https://doi.org/10.1016/j.comppsych.2017.12.006.
23. Baranyi G, Cassidy M, Fazel S, Priebe S, Mundt AP. Prevalence of posttraumatic stress disorder in prisoners. Epidemiol Rev. 2018;40(1):134–45. https://doi.org/10.1093/epirev/mxx015.
24. Briere J, Agee E, Dietrich A. Cumulative trauma and current posttraumatic stress disorder status in general population and inmate samples. Psychol Trauma Theory Res Pract Policy. 2016;8(4):439–46. https://doi.org/10.1037/tra0000107.
25. Chen M. Mass incarceration and adolescent development: connecting identity and trauma in Black adolescent males. Child Development Theses. Published online. 1 Nov 2018. https://digitalcommons.slc.edu/child_development_etd/25
26. Driessen M, Schroeder T, Widmann B, von Schönfeld CE, Schneider F. Childhood trauma, psychiatric disorders, and criminal behavior in Pris oners in Germany. J Clin Psychiatry. 2006;67(10):1486–92. https://doi.org/10.4088/jcp.v67n1001.
27. Cahn BR, Goodman MS, Peterson CT, Maturi R, Mills PJ. Yoga, Meditation and mind-body health: increased BDNF, cortisol awakening response, and altered inflammatory marker expression after a 3-month yoga and meditation retreat. Front Hum Neurosci 2017; 11. https://www.frontiersin.org/articles/10.3389/fnhum.2017.00315. Accessed 18 June 2023.
28. Chopin SM, Sheerin CM, Meyer BL. Yoga for warriors: an intervention for veterans with comorbid chronic pain and PTSD. Psychol Trauma Theory Res Pract Policy. 2020;12(8):888–96. https://doi.org/10.1037/tra0000649.
29. Davis LW, Schmid AA, Daggy JK, et al. Symptoms improve after a yoga program designed for PTSD in a randomized controlled trial with veterans and civilians. Psychol Trauma Theory Res Pract Policy. 2020;12(8):904–12. https://doi.org/10.1037/tra0000564.
30. Harner H, Henderer A, Murphy N. Trauma-informed yoga teacher training: impact on incarcerated men's wellness. Int J Yoga Ther. 2023;33 https://doi.org/10.17761/2023-d-22-00053.
31. Hanvey GA, et al. Proof-of-concept of an integrated yoga and psychological intervention in mitigating distress among diverse women with gynecologic, gastrointestinal, and thoracic cancers. Integr Cancer Ther. 2024; https://doi.org/10.1177/15347354241283113. Accessed 3 Dec 2024
32. Tenfelde SM, Hatchett L, Saban KL. "Maybe black girls do yoga": a focus group study with predominantly low-income African-American women. Complement Ther Med. 2018;40:230–5. https://doi.org/10.1016/j.ctim.2017.11.017.
33. Alim TN, Charney DS, Mellman TA. An overview of posttraumatic stress disorder in African Americans. J Clin Psychol. 2006;62(7):801–13. https://doi.org/10.1002/jclp.20280.

34. Allely CS, Allely B. Post traumatic stress disorder in incarcerated populations: current cl inical considerations and recommendations. JCP. 2020;10(1):30–42. https://doi.org/10.1108/jcp-09-2019-0044.
35. Stensrud RH, Gilbride DD, Bruinekool RM. The childhood to prison pipeline: early childhood trauma as reported by a prison population. Rehabil Couns Bull. 2019;62(4):195–208. https://doi.org/10.1177/0034355218774844.
36. Arditti JA, Savla J. Parental incarceration and child trauma symptoms in single caregiver homes. J Child Fam Stud. 2015;24(3):551–61. https://doi.org/10.1007/s10826-013-9867-2.
37. Craig SL, Austin A, Levenson J, Leung VWY, Eaton AD, D'Souza SA. Frequencies and patterns of adverse childhood events in LGBTQ+ youth. Child Abuse Negl. 2020;107:104623. https://doi.org/10.1016/j.chiabu.2020.104623.
38. Felitti VJ, Anda RF, Nordenberg D, et al. Relationship of childhood abuse and household dysfunction to many of the leading causes of death in adults: the adverse childhood experiences (ACE) study. Am J Prev Med. 1998;14(4):245–58. https://doi.org/10.1016/S0749-3797(98)00017-8.
39. Yoder JR, Whitaker K, Quinn CR. Perceptions of recidivism among incarcerated youth: the relationship between exposure to childhood trauma, mental health status, and the protective effect of mental health services in Juvenile justice settings. Adv Soc Work. 2017;18(1):250–69. https://doi.org/10.18060/21305.
40. Morrison M, Pettus C, Drake B, Roth K, Renn T. Trauma and incarceration: a latent class analysis of lifetime trauma exposures for individuals in prison. J Trauma Dissociation. 2024;25(2):168–84. https://doi.org/10.1080/15299732.2023.2289189.
41. Boland J, Rock R, Johnson AK, Jones MA, Salekin RT, Anderson JL. Pathways to incarceration: an examination of childhood maltreatment and personality psychopathology in incarcerated adults. Psychol Crime Law. 2021;27(3):253–64. https://doi.org/10.1080/1068316X.2020.1798426.
42. Dowell CM, Mejia GC, Preen DB, Segal L. Low birth weight and maternal incarceration in pregnancy: a longitudinal linked data study of Western Australian infants. SSM Popul Health. 2019;7:100324. https://doi.org/10.1016/j.ssmph.2018.11.008.
43. Zeman JL, Dallaire DH, Folk JB, Thrash TM. Maternal incarceration, children's psychological adjustment, and the mediating role of emotion regulation. J Abnorm Child Psychol. 2018;46(2):223–36. https://doi.org/10.1007/s10802-017-0275-8.
44. Giordano PC, Copp JE. 'Packages' of risk: implications for determining the effect of maternal incarceration on child wellbeing. Criminol Public Policy. 2015;14(1):157–68. https://doi.org/10.1111/1745-9133.12118.
45. Foster H. The strains of maternal imprisonment: importation and deprivation stressors for women and children. J Crim Just. 2012;40(3):221–9. https://doi.org/10.1016/j.jcrimjus.2012.01.005.
46. Lister RL, Drake W, Scott BH, Graves C. Black maternal mortality-the elephant in the room. World J Gynecol Womens Health. 2019;3(1) https://doi.org/10.33552/wjgwh.2019.03.000555.
47. Joseph KS, Boutin A, Lisonkova S, et al. Maternal mortality in the United States: recent trends, current status, and future considerations. Obstet Gynecol. 2021;137(5):763. https://doi.org/10.1097/AOG.0000000000004361.
48. Montalmant KE, Ettinger AK. The racial disparities in maternal mortality and impact of structural racism and implicit racial bias on pregnant Black women: a review of the literature. J Racial Ethn Health Disparities. 2024;11(6):3658–77. https://doi.org/10.1007/s40615-023-01816-x.
49. Singh GK. Trends and social inequalities in maternal mortality in the United States, 1969-2018. Int J MCH AIDS. 2021;10(1):29–42. https://doi.org/10.21106/ijma.444.
50. Spilsbury JC, Kahana S, Drotar D, Creeden R, Flannery DJ, Friedman S. Profiles of behavioral problems in children who witness domestic violence. Violence Vict. 2008;23(1):3–17. https://doi.org/10.1891/0886-6708.23.1.3.

51. Meltzer H, Doos L, Vostanis P, Ford T, Goodman R. The mental health of children who witness domestic violence. Child Fam Soc Work. 2009;14(4):491–501. https://doi.org/10.1111/j.1365-2206.2009.00633.x.
52. Dube SR, Anda RF, Felitti VJ, Chapman DP, Williamson DF, Giles WH. Childhood abuse, household dysfunction, and the risk of attempted suicide throughout the life span findings from the adverse childhood experiences study. JAMA. 2001;286(24):3089–96. https://doi.org/10.1001/jama.286.24.3089.
53. Burke NJ, Hellman JL, Scott BG, Weems CF, Carrion VG. The impact of adverse childhood experiences on an urban pediatric population. Child Abuse Negl. 2011;35(6):408–13. https://doi.org/10.1016/j.chiabu.2011.02.006.
54. Kallander EK, Weimand BM, Hanssen-Bauer K, Van Roy B, Ruud T. Factors associated with quality of life for children affected by parental illness or substance abuse. Scand J Caring Sci. 2021;35(2):405–19. https://doi.org/10.1111/scs.12868.
55. Lewis QJ, Smith BD, Offiong A, Prioleau M, Powell TW. When a house is never a home: housing instability among youth affected by parental drug abuse. Child Abuse Negl. 2021;118:105131. https://doi.org/10.1016/j.chiabu.2021.105131.
56. Bryan B. Housing instability following felony conviction and incarceration: disentangling being marked from being locked up. J Quant Criminol. 2023;39(4):833–74. https://doi.org/10.1007/s10940-022-09550-z.
57. Marcal KE. The impact of housing instability on child maltreatment: a causal investigation. J Fam Soc Work. 2018;21(4–5):331–47. https://doi.org/10.1080/10522158.2018.1469563.
58. Martin E. Hidden consequences: the impact of incarceration on dependent children. National Institute of Justice.
59. Martin MS, Eljdupovic G, McKenzie K, Colman I. Risk of violence by inmates with childhood trauma and mental health needs. Law Hum Behav. 2015;39(6):614–23. https://doi.org/10.1037/lhb0000149.
60. Persyn MK. "Mass Incarceration and Child Trauma" by Mary Kelly Persyn (July–September 2017 P&R Issue) - PRRAC — Connecting Research to Advocacy. July 5, 2017. https://www.prrac.org/mass-incarceration-and-child-trauma/. Accessed 30 Mar 2025.
61. Mallett CA. The school-to-prison pipeline: a critical review of the punitive paradigm shift. Child Adolesc Soc Work J. 2016;33(1):15–24. https://doi.org/10.1007/s10560-015-0397-1.
62. Skiba RJ, Arredondo MI, Williams NT. More than a metaphor: the contribution of exclusionary discipline to a school-to-prison pipeline. Equity Excell Educ. 2014;47(4):546–64. https://doi.org/10.1080/10665684.2014.958965.
63. Cuellar AE, Markowitz S. School suspension and the school-to-prison pipeline. Int Rev Law Econ. 2015;43:98–106. https://doi.org/10.1016/j.irle.2015.06.001.
64. Keisch DM, Scott T. U.S. education reform and the maintenance of white supremacy through structural violence. Published online 2015.
65. Schiff M. Can restorative justice disrupt the 'school-to-prison pipeline?'. Contemp Justice Rev. 2018;21(2):121–39. https://doi.org/10.1080/10282580.2018.1455509.
66. Payne YA, Brown TM. It's set up for failure, and they know this: how the school-to-prison pipeline impacts the educational experiences of street identified Black youth and young adults Martin Luther King, Jr. lecture. Vill L Rev. 2017;62(2):307–26.
67. DeFina R, Hannon L. The impact of mass incarceration on poverty. Crime Delinq. 2013;59(4) https://doi.org/10.1177/0011128708328864. Accessed 30 Mar 2025
68. Covin L Jr. Homelessness, poverty, and incarceration: the criminalization of despair. J Forensic Psychol Pract. 2012;12(5):439–56. https://doi.org/10.1080/15228932.2012.713835.
69. Rabuy B, Kopf D. Prisons of poverty: uncovering the pre-incarceration incomes of the imprisoned. Prison Policy Initiative. 2015; https://www.jstor.org/stable/resrep27310. Accessed 30 Mar 2025
70. Miller RR. Impacts of incarceration on the African American family. Routledge; 2020. https://doi.org/10.4324/9780203789001.

71. Keene DE, Smoyer AB, Blankenship KM. Stigma, housing and identity after prison. Sociol Rev. 2018; https://journals.sagepub.com/doi/abs/10.1177/0038026118777447?journalCode=sora. Accessed 17 June 2023
72. Muentner L, Holder N, Burnson C, Runion H, Weymouth L, Poehlmann-Tynan J. Jailed parents and their young children: residential instability, homelessness, and behavior problems. J Child Fam Stud. 2019;28(2):370–86. https://doi.org/10.1007/s10826-018-1265-3.
73. Rios VM. The hyper-criminalization of Black and Latino male youth in the era of mass incarceration. Souls. 2006;8(2):40–54. https://doi.org/10.1080/10999940600680457.
74. Rios VM. Punished: policing the lives of Black and Latino boys. NYU Press; 2011.
75. Jahn JL, Agenor M, Chen JT, Krieger N. Frequent police stops, parental incarceration and mental health: results among US non-Hispanic Black and white adolescent girls and boys. J Epidemiol Community Health. 2021;75(7):658–64. https://doi.org/10.1136/jech-2020-214578.
76. Vaughans KC, Harris L. The police, Black and Hispanic boys: a dangerous inability to Mentalize. J Infant Child Adolesc Psychother. 2016;15(3):171–8. https://doi.org/10.1080/15289168.2016.1214454.
77. Vaughans KC. Black boys in the eye of the storm. Psychoanal Study Child. 2021;74(1):47–58. https://doi.org/10.1080/00797308.2020.1859300.
78. Ramaswamy M. Progressive paths to masculinity for young Black and Latino men in an urban alternatives-to-incarceration program. West J Black Stud. 2010;34(4):412–24.
79. Farber D. The war on drugs: a history. NYU Press; 2021.
80. Hattery AJ, Smith E. Policing Black bodies: how Black lives are surveilled and how to work for change. Rowman & Littlefield; 2021.
81. Jones-Brown D, Williams JM. Over-policing Black bodies: the need for multidimensional and transformative reforms. J Ethn Crim Justice. 2021;19(3–4):181–7. https://doi.org/10.1080/15377938.2021.1992326.
82. Barazzone N, Santos I, McGowan J, Donaghay-Spire E. The links between adult attachment and post-traumatic stress: a systematic review. Psychol Psychother. 2018;92(1):131–47. https://doi.org/10.1111/papt.12181.
83. Pearlman LA, Courtois CA. Clinical applications of the attachment framework: relational treatment of complex trauma. J Traum Stress. 2005;18(5):449–59. https://doi.org/10.1002/jts.20052.
84. Schore AN. Relational trauma and the developing right brain: the neurobiology of broken attachment bonds. In: Relational trauma in infancy. Routledge; 2009.
85. Schore A. Affect dysregulation & disorders of the self. W W Norton & Co; 2003. Published online
86. van der Kolk BA, Pelcovitz D, Roth S, Mandel FS, McFarlane A, Herman JL. Dissociation, somatization, and affect dysregulation: the complexity of adaptation of trauma. AJP. 1996;153(7):83–93. https://doi.org/10.1176/ajp.153.7.83.
87. Beauchaine TP, Cicchetti D. Emotion dysregulation and emerging psychopathology: a transdiagnostic, transdisciplinary perspective. Dev Psychopathol. 2019;31(3):799–804. https://doi.org/10.1017/s0954579419000671.
88. Garofalo C, Holden CJ, Zeigler-Hill V, Velotti P. Understanding the connection between self-esteem and aggression: the mediating role of emotion dysregulation. Aggress Behav. 2016;42(1):3–15. https://doi.org/10.1002/ab.21601.
89. Shea A, Walsh C, MacMillan H, Steiner M. Child maltreatment and HPA axis dysregulation: relationship to major d epressive disorder and post traumatic stress disorder in females. Psychoneuroendocrinology. 2005;30(2):162–78. https://doi.org/10.1016/j.psyneuen.2004.07.001.
90. Owen-Smith A, Black H, Emerson D, et al. A pilot study to adapt a trauma-informed, mindfulness-based yoga intervention for Justice-involved youth. Int J Yoga Ther. 2021;31(1) Article_18 https://doi.org/10.17761/2021-D-21-00032.

91. Justice L, Brems C, Ehlers K. Bridging body and mind: considerations for trauma-informed yoga. Int J Yoga Ther. 2018;28(1):39–50. https://doi.org/10.17761/2018-00017R2.
92. Nicotera N, Viggiano E. A pilot study of a trauma-informed yoga and mindfulness intervention with young women incarcerated in the juvenile justice system. J Addict Offender Couns. 2021;42(2):80–96. https://doi.org/10.1002/jaoc.12095.
93. Gerritsen RJS, Band GPH. Breath of life: the respiratory vagal stimulation model of contemplative activity. Front Hum Neurosci. 2018:12. https://www.frontiersin.org/articles/10.3389/fnhum.2018.00397. Accessed 18 June 2023
94. Denson TF. Breaking the cycle of violent crime and punishment: the promise of neuronormalization. Soc Issues Policy Rev. 2021;15(1):237–76. https://doi.org/10.1111/sipr.12076.
95. Choi Y, Kim M, Park J. Mental healthcare through cognitive emotional regulation strategies among prisoners. Healthcare. 2024;12(1):6. https://doi.org/10.3390/healthcare12010006.
96. Walsh K, Gonsalves VM, Scalora MJ, King S, Hardyman PL. Child maltreatment histories among female inmates reporting inmate on inmate sexual victimization in prison: the mediating role of emotion dysregulation. J Interpers Violence. 2012;27(3):492–512. https://doi.org/10.1177/0886260511421670.
97. Baskin-Sommers AR, Fonteneau K. Correctional change through neuroscience symposium: criminal behavior and the brain: when law and neuroscience collide. Fordham L Rev. 2016;85(2):423–36.
98. Rousseau D, Long N, Jackson E, Jurgensen J. Empowering through embodied awareness: evaluation of a peer-facilitate d trauma-informed mindfulness curriculum in a woman's prison. Prison J. 2019;99(4_suppl):14S–37S. https://doi.org/10.1177/0032885519860546.
99. Joseph VW, Moniz-Lewis DIK, Richards DK, Pearson MR, Luoma JB, Witkiewitz K. Internalized shame among justice-involved women in substance use disorder treatment: measurement invariance and changes during treatment. Stigma and Health. 2024;9(3):303–10. https://doi.org/10.1037/sah0000427.
100. Martínez-Falquina S. Re-mapping the trauma paradigm: the politics of native American grief in Louise Erdrich's "Shamengwa". In: Martínez-Alfaro MJ, Pellicer-Ortín S, editors. Memory frictions in contemporary literature. Springer International Publishing; 2017. p. 209–30. https://doi.org/10.1007/978-3-319-61759-6_11.
101. Collins PH. Black feminist thought, 30th anniversary edition: knowledge, consciousness, and the politics of empowerment. Routledge; 2022. https://doi.org/10.4324/9781003245650.
102. Crenshaw KW. Mapping the margins: intersectionality, identity politics, and violence against women of color. In: The public nature of private violence. Routledge; 1994.
103. Saha S, Komaromy M, Koepsell TD, Bindman AB. Patient-physician racial concordance and the perceived quality and use of health care. Arch Intern Med. 1999;159(9):997–1004. https://doi.org/10.1001/archinte.159.9.997.
104. Cooper LA, Roter DL, Johnson RL, Ford DE, Steinwachs DM, Powe NR. Patient-centered communication, ratings of care, and concordance of patient and physician race. Ann Intern Med. 2003;139(11):907–15. https://doi.org/10.7326/0003-4819-139-11-200312020-00009.
105. Gone JP. Redressing first nations historical trauma: theorizing mechanisms for indigenous culture as mental health treatment. Transcult Psychiatry. 2013;50(5):683–706. https://journals-sagepub-com.ucsf.idm.oclc.org/doi/full/10.1177/1363461513487669. Accessed 26 May 2025
106. Hardy KV. Race through a trauma lens. In: Promoting cultural sensitivity in supervision. Routledge; 2017.
107. Menakem R. My grandmother's hands: racialized trauma and the pathway to mending our hearts and bodies. Central Recovery Press; 2017.
108. Metzl JM, Hansen H. Structural competency: theorizing a new medical engagement with stigma and inequality. Soc Sci Med. 2014;103:126–33. https://doi.org/10.1016/j.socscimed.2013.06.032.

109. Embodiment and social justice: a conversation with Reverend Angel Kyodo Williams and Dr. Scott Lyons; 2021. https://www.youtube.com/watch?v=dgnxBTvNK1U. Accessed 17 June 2023.
110. Johnson R. Embodied social justice. Taylor & Francis; 2022.
111. Johnson R. Oppression embodied: the intersecting dimensions of trauma, oppression, and somatic psychology. The USA Body Psychother J. 2009;8(1):19–31.
112. Cloud DH, Williams B, Haardöerfer R, Hosbey JT, Cooper HLF. Self-injury and the embodiment of solitary confinement among adult men in Louisiana prisons. SSM - Popul Health. 2023;22:101354. https://doi.org/10.1016/j.ssmph.2023.101354.
113. Leuzinger-Bohleber M. Finding the body in the mind: embodied memories, trauma, and depression. Routledge; 2018.
114. van der Kaap-Deeder J, Audenaert E, Vandevelde S, et al. Choosing when choices are limited: the role of perceived afforded choice and autonomy in prisoners' well-being. Law Hum Behav. 2017;41(6):567–78. https://doi.org/10.1037/lhb0000259.
115. DeHart D, Iachini AL. Mental Health & Trauma among incarcerated persons: development of a training curriculum for correctional officers. Am J Crim Just. 2019;44(3):457–73. https://doi.org/10.1007/s12103-019-9473-y.
116. De Giorgi A. Back to nothing: prisoner reentry and neoliberal neglect. Social Justice. 2017;44(1):83–120.
117. Hughes TA, James DJ. Reentry Trends in the United States | Bureau of Justice Statistics. October 2002. https://bjs.ojp.gov/library/publications/reentry-trends-united-states. Accessed 5 Feb 2025.
118. Wikoff N, Linhorst DM, Morani N. Recidivism among participants of a reentry program for prisoners released without supervision. Soc Work Res. 2012;36(4):289–99. https://doi.org/10.1093/swr/svs021.
119. Davidson RJ, McEwen BS. Social influences on neuroplasticity: stress and interventions to promote well-being. Nat Neurosci. 2012;15(5):689–95. https://doi.org/10.1038/nn.3093.
120. Burnett-Zeigler I, Hong S, Waldron EM, Maletich C, Yang A, Moskowitz J. A mindfulness-based intervention for low-income African American women with depressive symptoms delivered by an experienced instructor versus a novice instructor. J Altern Complement Med. 2019;25(7):699–708. https://doi.org/10.1089/acm.2018.0393.
121. Garfin DR, Amador A, Osorio J, Ruivivar KS, Torres A, Nyamathi AM. Adaptation of a mindfulness-based intervention for trauma-exposed, unhoused women with substance use disorder. Psychol Trauma Theory Res Pract Policy. 2024;16(Suppl 3):S599–610. https://doi.org/10.1037/tra0001486.
122. Adhikari K. Study of effect of *Vipassana* on anxiety and depression. IJPBS. 2012;2(6):274–6. https://doi.org/10.5923/j.ijpbs.20120206.11.
123. Nemeroff R, Moura F, Jeffers M, Hitchcock S. Yoga as a treatment intervention for anxiety-spectrum disorders. Pract Innov. 2024;9(2):119–31. https://doi.org/10.1037/pri0000226.
124. Johnson JE, Stout RL, Miller TR, et al. Randomized cost-effectiveness trial of group interpersonal psychotherapy (IPT) for prisoners with major depression. J Consult Clin Psychol. 2019;87(4):392–406. https://doi.org/10.1037/ccp0000379.
125. Bouw N, Huijbregts SCJ, Scholte E, Swaab H. Mindfulness-based stress reduction in prison: experiences of inmates, instructors, and prison staff. Int J Offender Ther Comp Criminol. 2019;63(15–16):2550–71. https://doi.org/10.1177/0306624X19856232.
126. Taren AA, Gianaros PJ, Greco CM, et al. Mindfulness meditation training alters stress-related amygdala resting state functional connectivity: a randomized controlled trial. Soc Cogn Affect Neurosci. 2015;10(12):1758–68. https://doi.org/10.1093/scan/nsv066.
127. Payne P, Levine PA, Crane-Godreau MA. Somatic experiencing: using interoception and proprioception as core e lements of trauma therapy. Front Psychol. 2015:6. https://doi.org/10.3389/fpsyg.2015.00093.

128. Yoga as an adjunctive treatment for posttraumatic stress disorder: a randomized controlled trial. Psychiatrist.com. https://www.psychiatrist.com/jcp/yoga-adjunctive-treatment-posttraumatic-stress-disorder/. Accessed 30 Mar 2025.
129. Xu W, Itagi RK, Thaiyar MS. Impact of Yama and Niyama on Psychospiritual factors in young adults: a randomized controlled trial. J Appl Conscious Stud. 2021;9(1):32. https://doi.org/10.4103/ijoyppp.ijoyppp_17_20.
130. Khalsa SB, Cohen L, McCall T, Telles S, Cramer H. The principles and practice of yoga in health care. 2nd ed. Jessica Kingsley Publishers; 2024.
131. Givens J. Essential pranayama: breathing techniques for balance, healing, and peace. Sourcebooks, Inc.; 2020.
132. Sunita Y. Pranayama yoga: the art of relaxation. Lotus & the Rose; 1982.
133. BKS I. Yoga: the path to holistic health. Penguin; 2013.
134. Novaes MM, Palhano-Fontes F, Onias H, et al. Effects of yoga respiratory practice (Bhastrika pranayama) on anxiety, affect, and brain functional connectivity and activity: a randomized controlled trial. Front Psych. 2020:11. https://doi.org/10.3389/fpsyt.2020.00467.
135. Haller H, Mitzinger D, Cramer H. The integration of yoga breathing techniques in cognitive behavioral therapy for post-traumatic stress disorder: a pragmatic randomized controlled trial. Front Psych. 2023:14. https://doi.org/10.3389/fpsyt.2023.1101046.
136. Carter J, Gerbarg PL, Brown RP, Ware RS, D'Ambrosio C, et al. Multi-component yoga breath program for Vietnam veteran post traumatic stress disorder: randomized controlled trial. J Trauma Stress Disor Treat. 2013;02(03) https://doi.org/10.4172/2324-8947.1000108.
137. Adler S, Chao M. Integrative health equity: definition, principles, strategies, and reflections. Published online 2024.
138. Chao MT, Adler SR. Integrative medicine and the imperative for health justice. J Altern Complement Med. 2018;24(2):101–3. https://doi.org/10.1089/acm.2017.29042.mtc.
139. Kalsched D. Trauma and the soul: a psycho-spiritual approach to human development and its interruption. Routledge; 2013. https://books.google.com/books?id=Z6lpuQAACAAJ
140. Witkiewitz, K., Marlatt, G. A., & Walker, D. (2005). Mindfulness-Based Relapse Prevention for Alcohol and Substance Use Disorders. Journal of Cognitive Psychotherapy, 19(3), 211–228. https://doi.org/10.1891/jcop.2005.19.3.211

MIX
Papier aus verantwortungsvollen Quellen
Paper from responsible sources
FSC® C105338

If you have any concerns about our products,
you can contact us on
ProductSafety@springernature.com

In case Publisher is established outside the EU,
the EU authorized representative is:
Springer Nature Customer Service Center GmbH
Europaplatz 3, 69115 Heidelberg, Germany

Printed by Libri Plureos GmbH
in Hamburg, Germany